J⦿BS
steve
thinking differently

JOBS
steve
thinking differently

BY PATRICIA LAKIN

Aladdin

NEW YORK   LONDON   TORONTO   SYDNEY   NEW DELHI

For Lee, with love

—P. L.

ALADDIN

An imprint of Simon & Schuster Children's Publishing Division

1230 Avenue of the Americas, New York, NY 10020

First Aladdin paperback edition February 2012

Copyright © 2011 by Patricia Lakin

All rights reserved, including the right of reproduction

in whole or in part in any form.

ALADDIN is a trademark of Simon & Schuster, Inc., and related logo

is a registered trademark of Simon & Schuster, Inc.

Also available in an Aladdin hardcover edition.

For information about special discounts for bulk purchases,

please contact Simon & Schuster Special Sales at 1-866-506-1949

or business@simonandschuster.com.

The Simon & Schuster Speakers Bureau can bring authors to your live event.

For more information or to book an event contact the Simon & Schuster Speakers Bureau

at 1-866-248-3049 or visit our website at www.simonspeakers.com.

Designed by Karina Granda

The text of this book was set in Adobe Caslon Pro.

Manufactured in the United States of America 0112 OFF

2 4 6 8 10 9 7 5 3 1

Full CIP data for this book is available from the Library of Congress.

ISBN 978-1-4424-5394-4 (hc)

ISBN 978-1-4424-5393-7 (pbk)

ISBN 978-1-4424-5349-4 (eBook)

contents

"CLICK.
BOOM.
AMAZING!"

— STEVE JOBS
(MACWORLD EXPO, 2006)

introduction
CONNECTING THE DOTS

How did a young boy who was a little terror in elementary school, a first-class prankster, and a college dropout grow up to become a man who not only led one of the world's most innovative companies but was also revered for his brilliant creations?

By following his passions, Steve Jobs created one world-famous company, Apple Inc., and nurtured another, Pixar Studios. Along the way, he revolutionized home computers and the music and telephone industries and helped bring computer-animated films like *Toy Story* and *WALL-E* to life. With a team of technical artists like himself, he produced the iPod, the iPhone, and the iPad.

Perhaps Steve would say it's because he connected the dots in his life.

As an adult, he said of those dots, "You can only connect them looking backwards. So you have to trust that the dots will somehow connect in your future. You have to trust in something—your gut, destiny, life, karma. . . . And most important, have the courage to follow your heart and intuition."

1

BEGINNINGS

GIVING UP A CHILD FOR ADOPTION has to be an extraordinarily difficult and heart-wrenching decision. But in 1955, one particular couple felt they had no choice.

Abdulfattah "John" Jandali and Joanne Scheible were graduate students at the University of Wisconsin who wanted desperately to complete their education. They believed their studies would end, their subsequent careers would be nonexistent, if they chose to keep their child. And so, in San Francisco,

California, on February 24, 1955, when their baby boy was born, they put him up for adoption.

Joanne Scheible, the baby's birth mother, felt strongly that the adoptive parents had to be college graduates. Her first choice was a lawyer and his wife. But that couple wanted a girl.

The next family on the adoption agency's list was Clara and Paul Jobs. They were delighted to adopt either a boy or a girl and open their home and their hearts to this infant.

The Jobses—unbeknownst to Joanna Scheible at first—were not college graduates. Clara Jobs had only finished high school. She worked as an accountant. Paul Jobs hadn't even completed high school. He had served in the coast guard during World War II and worked as a machinist.

When Joanne Scheible discovered that the Jobses weren't college graduates, she revised her conditions: In order for the adoption to go through, they had to promise they would send the child to college. The Jobses simply wanted to nurture and love their baby boy. How they would pay for his education was a question they would tackle in the future. But promise they did. Papers were signed and the adoption became official. A family was born. They named their son Steven Paul Jobs.

At the time of the adoption, Paul and Clara lived in a small apartment in San Francisco. Soon after Steven came into their lives, they moved to an inexpensive rental home in South San Francisco. In 1958 the Jobses added to their family once again when they adopted a baby girl, whom they named Patty.

In 1960, when Steve was five, Paul's job transfer brought his family to a modest three-bedroom rental house in Mountain View, California—a new suburban area south of San Francisco, where small houses and new businesses were quickly developing.

Steve was inquisitive, energetic, and imaginative. As a toddler, he often woke up at four o'clock in the morning. To make sure they could get their rest, his parents bought him a rocking horse to play with. They also put a phonograph in his room with records by Little Richard, a rock-and-roll singer popular in the 1950s. Maybe Little Richard was their favorite artist and that's why they chose his music. But it was an interesting choice: Little Richard's songs, from "Good Golly, Miss Molly" to "Tutti Frutti," were fast-paced and *loud*—not exactly music to relax to. During those few early morning hours, their son could safely "rock" in more ways than one.

Many women in the 1950s were stay-at-home mothers, and Steve was fortunate that Clara was able to spend a great deal of time with him, even teaching him to read before he started school. When not at work, Paul was a constant presence in Steve's life too.

"I was very lucky. . . . My father, Paul, was a pretty remarkable man. . . . He was a machinist by trade and worked very hard and was kind of a genius with his hands. . . . He . . . showed me how to use a hammer and saw and how to build things. It really was very good for me. He spent a lot of time with me."

Paul had a workbench in his garage, and when Steve was about five or six years old, his father sectioned off a part of it for him. "Steve, this is your workbench now," he said. He kept his tools and workbench clean and in perfect order, and while many parents might have been reluctant to let a young child "invade their space," Paul welcomed Steve to share his tools, his space, and his own joy in creating.

Paul liked to buy old cars, fix them up, and sell them. Refurbishing those cars gave him some experience working with a car's electronics parts and exposed Steve to the auto's inner workings. Paul passed along not only his fascination with electronics but also his pride in workmanship. He often told his son that when building something, every part should be well made and put together with precision and care, whether the part showed or not.

Steve said of his father, "He can fix anything and make it work and take any mechanical thing apart and get it back together. That was my first glimpse of it. I started to gravitate more toward electronics, and he used to get me things I could take apart and put back together."

Even though Steve knew how to read and build things when he started at Monta Loma Elementary

School in Mountain View, it was still a difficult time for him. "School was pretty hard for me at the beginning. . . . When I got there I really just wanted to do two things: I wanted to read books, because I loved reading books, and I wanted to go outside and chase butterflies. You know, do the things that five-year-olds like to do."

It's possible he didn't have teachers who knew how to reach—or teach—him. And it's possible that the controlled, structured environment—having to sit still at a desk from early morning until midafternoon—was uninviting and a challenge for Steve. He said of that time, "I encountered authority of a different kind than I had ever encountered before, and I did not like it. And they really almost got me. They came close to really beating any curiosity out of me."

Also, Steve was a bit of a loner, used to getting his own way. When something didn't go as he wished at home, he'd storm off and cry. Those qualities may have made it more difficult for him to fit in with his classmates at school. His way of dealing with the day-to-day life at school that he thought was boring and a waste of his time was to make mischief. Lots of it.

In third grade Steve's partner in crime was his buddy Rick Ferrentino. They let snakes loose in the classroom and set explosives off in the teacher's desk. With Rick, more complex pranks were possible.

Outside the school, all the kids' bikes were lined up and locked in the bike racks. Steve and Rick found out who owned each bike and traded their own bike lock combinations for that person's combination. When they amassed all the combinations for each of the bike locks, they went into action.

They opened every bike lock and reattached it to someone else's bike. When school was dismissed and the kids went to open their locks, they couldn't figure out why their locks weren't opening. Steve recalled the outcome years later: "It took them until about ten o'clock that night to get all the bikes sorted out."

In fourth grade the principal was determined to separate the two boys. By chance, Mrs. Imogene "Teddy" Hill, who taught an advanced fourth-grade class, volunteered to take one of the boys. She was assigned to be Steve's teacher. He would later remember her as "one of the other saints of my life."

Imogene Hill followed her own instincts growing up. At the age of three, she acted onstage and went by the name "Little Imogene." She was part of a sister-and-brother dancing act and was described as being a bundle of energy. She kept up her love of acting even in college.

She was now a married woman and a dedicated teacher. Perhaps her love of theater and performing made her an unorthodox teacher. Or perhaps she was simply a passionate teacher who wanted to inspire every student in her classroom. Whatever it was, she must have been sizing up this particular fourth-grade boy to figure out how to reach him.

After the first few weeks of school, she approached Steve with a challenge: If he took a math workbook home, completed it all on his own, and got 80 percent of it correct, she'd give him a huge lollipop *and* five dollars. Steve responded. He accepted the challenge, succeeded, and got the candy and the five dollars. He said, "She got hip to my whole situation in about a month and kindled a passion in me for learning things."

As Jobs recalled, "She got me kits for making cameras. I ground my own lens and made a camera. . . . I think I probably learned more academically that one year than I've ever learned in my life."

Fourth grade with Mrs. Hill has to be considered a turning point in Steve's life. In a 1995 interview he said, "I'm a hundred percent sure that if it hadn't been for Mrs. Hill in fourth grade and a few others, I absolutely would have ended up in jail. I could see those tendencies in myself to have a certain energy to do something. It could have been directed at doing something interesting that other people thought was a good idea or doing something interesting that other people maybe didn't like so much." He went on to say, "When you're young, a little bit of course correction goes a long way."

At the end of the school year, Steve had done so well academically that the administrators had him tested. He scored so high that the school system wanted to advance this former troublemaker directly to high school.

Luckily for Steve, his parents thought sending an eleven-year-old to high school was a terrible idea. They agreed to have him skip one grade (fifth) but no more than that. So, in the fall of 1966, Steve entered sixth grade at Crittenden Middle School in Mountain View.

2

LEARNING IN A GARAGE

OUNTAIN VIEW GAVE STEVE A plethora of educational opportunities outside of school. It was a place where Steve, with his intellect and single-minded interest in anything electrical and electronic, could feed his curiosity.

In order to understand how and why the Jobses' neighborhood and the surrounding area was so important and influential to Steve's development, it's necessary to go back to the year after Steve was born—1956.

This was the year that scientist William Bradford Shockley, along with John Bardeen and Walter H. Brattain, won the Nobel Prize in Physics "for their researches on semiconductors and their discovery of the transistor effect." A transistor is the fundamental building block of modern electronic devices. It revolutionized the electronics field and paved the way for smaller and less expensive radios, calculators, and computers.

Shortly after winning the Nobel Prize, Shockley moved back to his hometown of Palo Alto, in the valley area south of San Francisco. He was to head a company called Shockley Semiconductor Laboratory, which was to be located in Mountain View. One of the products they worked on was this relatively new device—a transistor. Shockley was at the forefront of using silicon as a semiconductor for these transistors.

Shockley's company stood alongside other institutions and companies that were starting out or already based nearby. This northern spot in California was an ideal location for burgeoning industries. The United

PATRICIA LAKIN

States government's space program, NASA (National Aeronautics and Space Administration), was also in high gear at this time. Lockheed, the aeronautics firm and a major NASA contractor, had a significant presence in this part of the country. And two famous local men, Bill Hewlett and Dave Packard (who started their business in a garage), located their electronics company, Hewlett-Packard, in Palo Alto.

As business boomed, young professionals—professors, engineers, designers, electricians, and scientists—were moving into the area in droves. A few years earlier, Mountain View and its surrounding valley communities had been blooming with apricot orchards. Now they were blooming with new businesses and new housing.

One young, newly married engineer moved onto Steve's Mountain View street, just a few houses away. His name was Larry Lang, and Steve gravitated to him when he was about twelve years old. Steve described their introduction: "There was a man that moved in down the street . . . with his wife, and it turned out he was an engineer at Hewlett-Packard and he was a ham radio operator and really into electronics. What he did to get to know the kids in the block was rather a strange thing. He put out a carbon microphone and a battery and a speaker on his driveway, where you could talk into the microphone and your voice would be amplified in the speaker."

Steve's father had taught him that in order for a voice to be amplified, an amplifier was needed. So Jobs raced home to tell his dad what he'd just witnessed—an amplified voice *with no amplifier*. Father and son argued back and forth until Steve dragged his dad down the block so he could show him Lang's microphone. Even Steve's father learned something new that day.

After that initial introduction, Steve spent a great deal of time with Lang in his electronics-workshop garage. In a 1995 interview he recalled Lang's influence: "He taught me a lot of electronics too. . . . He used to build Heathkits. . . . Heathkits were these products that you would buy in kit form. You'd actually pay more money for them than you would if you just went and bought the finished product if it was available. These Heathkits would come with detailed manuals on how to put this thing together and all the parts would be laid out in a certain way and color coded. You'd actually build this thing yourself. I would say that gave one several things. It gave one an understanding of what was inside a finished product and how it worked, because it would include a theory of operation. But maybe even more importantly, it gave one the sense that one could build the things that one saw around oneself in the universe. These things were not mysteries anymore. I mean, you looked at a television set, you would think, 'Well, I haven't built one of those, but I could.'"

Jobs went on to say, "Things became much more clear . . . not these magical things that just appeared in one's environment, that one had no knowledge of their interiors. It gave one a tremendous degree of self-confidence, that through exploration and learning one could understand seemingly very complex things in one's environment. My childhood was very fortunate in that way."

Lang's influence went beyond what Steve learned

by hanging out in his neighbor's garage workshop. The engineer was also able to arrange for Steve to join Hewlett-Packard's Explorer Club in 1967.

The Explorer Club was open to budding adolescent engineers and met every Tuesday evening in the company cafeteria. At that time, firms like Hewlett-Packard were only too happy to share with young people all the new technologies and products they were developing. Various engineers from Hewlett-Packard would describe their latest projects—calculators, lasers, holograms, and the like. Jobs remembered one particular meeting: "They showed us one of their new desktop computers and let us play on it. I wanted one badly. . . . I just thought they were neat. I just wanted to mess around with one."

It's important to remember that when Steve Jobs was growing up, computers weren't found in people's homes. The first computers were originally created to produce error-free, speedy mathematical calculations, for use in laboratories and universities. They were massive contraptions, and they generated so much heat they had to be stored in designated rooms, kept cool so that the computers wouldn't overheat.

Desktop computers began to be developed in the early 1950s. Heathkit even created a kit to build one toward the end of the decade. In 1972 Hewlett-Packard introduced a desktop computer, which was considered a programmable calculator and was marketed to scientists and engineers.

Unfortunately, what was intriguing to Steve in the "outside" world was not in the curriculum at Crittenden Middle School. His sixth-grade classroom was nothing like Larry Lang's garage or Hewlett-Packard's cafeteria with scientists and engineers.

His new school wasn't a happy place for eleven-year-old Steve. He was now officially called "gifted." But instead of being placed with similarly gifted kids his own age, he was put in a classroom with kids far older. The school system didn't offer any help in trying to ease his adjustment, and to make matters worse, there was an element of kids at school who were serious troublemakers. According to one Steve Jobs biographer, "The police were often called to the school to break up fights. The situation was basically out of control. For Steve, who was extremely bright but also a little wild, an environment where his wildness went unnoticed in all the commotion, as did his intelligence, was a prescription for unhappiness."

Jobs was so bullied and miserable at Crittenden that one summer day before he was to enter seventh grade, he told his parents he refused to return to that school. He'd have to change schools or he'd simply stop attending any school.

Legally, Steve wouldn't have been allowed to quit school. But Paul and Clara Jobs knew his threat could cause them problems—not least of which was their promise (when they adopted him) to send their son to college. The obvious choice was to change schools. Changing schools meant changing communities.

Since Steve's birth, Paul and Clara had already moved from San Francisco to its southern suburbs on two separate occasions. Would they consider moving yet again?

They did, and for two reasons. First, they were used to taking their son's threats seriously. Second,

Patty (who was three years younger than Steve) would soon be attending Crittenden Middle School. Steve's experiences influenced his parents' decision to find a better school environment for both children.

In 1967 the Jobs family moved farther south to another San Francisco valley suburb, Los Altos. Their three-bedroom home brought the family closer to Paul's job. And it put Steve into the Cupertino school system, a district that at the time had a far better reputation than Mountain View. Los Altos was also considered to be part of the booming high-tech area.

In January of 1971, just five years after the Jobs family moved to Los Altos, this California valley area was given a nickname by Don Hoefler, a writer for a weekly trade paper, *Electronic News*. Thinking of the element that Shockley used in his transistors, he dubbed the area Silicon Valley, the name by which it's still known today.

Now that he was enrolled in a better school—Cupertino Junior High—Steve's school life should have been better. It wasn't. Steve was a year younger than the other kids in his grade. Although he was grouped with kids who were on his same intellectual level, he still didn't mix easily with his classmates.

He wasn't very interested in sports or being part of any team, which can be ways to make new friends. His only physical activity was swimming at his old community's Mountain View Dolphins Swim Club. But swimming isn't really a team sport, and Steve remained a loner—at least with kids his own age.

Fortunately, he did make a friend—Bill Fernandez. He was also a bit of a loner and older than Steve, but in the same class at Cupertino Junior High. He too was uninterested in sports. His garage, like many in this neighborhood, was a well-stocked electronic workshop. Bill's house was on Steve's route home from school and was a frequent after-school stopping place for him.

With their shared interest in electronics, Steve and Bill became close friends. On one occasion, Bill introduced Steve to a family that lived across the street from the Fernandez family—the Wozniaks. Jerry Wozniak had been teaching Bill what he knew about electronics. Jerry shared his technical knowledge with not only his own children but other interested children in the neighborhood. That was a common practice of engineers in the Los Altos area.

Bill told Steve about Jerry's oldest son, an electrical and electronics whiz kid who was also named Steve. Eighteen-year-old Steve Wozniak was born in 1950, five years before Steve Jobs. "Woz," as he was known, was already deeply involved in electronics; he'd been making drawings of computer designs for a while and hung out at the Stanford University library poring over technical books.

Woz recalled their meeting: "I remember Steve and I just sat on the sidewalk in front of Bill's house for the longest time, just sharing stories—mostly about pranks we'd pulled, and also what kind of electronic designs we'd done. It felt like we had so much in common. Typically, it was really hard for me to explain to people the kind of design stuff I worked on, but Steve got it right away. And I liked him. He was kind of skinny and wiry and full of energy."

Bill and Steve were more involved in projects such as working with lasers and bouncing their beams off

Steve Jobs: Thinking Differently

mirrors. They enjoyed watching the mirrors reflect those beams of light onto the walls.

Steve continued to attend Hewlett-Packard's Explorer Club on Tuesday nights. At one point, when he was about twelve or thirteen, he decided he wanted to build a frequency counter, a device that would track how often a certain electrical frequency occurred in a circuit. But Steve discovered as he was building that he needed some very specific parts.

What he did next was nervy, bold, ingenious, and for Steve, perfectly logical and reasonable: "I picked up the phone and called Bill Hewlett—he was listed in the Palo Alto phone book. He answered the phone and he was real nice. He chatted with me for twenty minutes. He didn't know me at all, but he ended up giving me some parts, and he got me a job that summer working at Hewlett-Packard on the line, assembling frequency counters. Assembling may be too strong. I was putting in screws. It didn't matter; I was in heaven."

3

HIGHER EDUCATION

STEVE STARTED AT HOMESTEAD High School in 1968. It was a time of major social, cultural, and political change in the United States: Civil rights leader Martin Luther King Jr. was assassinated in April, and two months later presidential candidate (and brother of the late president John F. Kennedy) Robert F. Kennedy met the same fate; thought-provoking films like Stanley Kubrick's *2001: A Space Odyssey* and the Beatles' *Yellow Submarine* played in movie theaters, while irreverent shows such as *Rowan & Martin's Laugh-In* and *The Smothers Brothers Comedy Hour* were on network television. Top songs were the Beatles' "Hey Jude" and Simon and Garfunkel's "Mrs. Robinson," and the war in Vietnam, which was costing American troops casualties and deaths, touched everyone's life and led to increasingly vocal public criticism. Antiwar protest groups were organized on college campuses and in high schools.

Along with these events, young people were exploring new ways of thinking about life and the world around them. A generation gap between parents and their children was emerging, as kids began questioning what their parents and the established society believed.

San Francisco became a destination for free-thinking young people (some called themselves "hippies") who were part of this counterculture.

For Steve, following one's dream (or doing one's own thing) wasn't considered quite so weird anymore. And in this community, filled with so many technical businesses, being caught up in electronics wasn't considered so weird anymore either.

At Homestead High, there was a popular class for just such "wireheads" (as these dedicated electronic fans like Steve were called): John McCollum's Electronics 1 course. McCollum had been Steve Wozniak's teacher, and Woz encouraged Bill and Steve to take the class together. McCollum was a former navy pilot who was probably accustomed to having his students follow his strict rules.

In his class, Steve may have felt that sense of the unbending authority figure coming back into his life. Despite the fact that he could have benefitted from the knowledge McCollum provided, he wasn't happy, and McCollum didn't seem happy with Steve, either. He later said, "He kind of faded into the background. He was usually off in a corner doing something on his own and really didn't want to have much of anything to do with either me or the rest of the class."

By the end of his sophomore year, Steve decided not to take McCollum's course the next year. He was becoming more interested in his classes in literature. He spent time reading poetry, listening to music, seeing movies, and paying more attention to girls. "I discovered Shakespeare, Dylan Thomas and all that classic stuff. I read *Moby-Dick* and went back as a junior taking creative-writing classes."

During that school year, once again, Steve took advantage of his neighborhood to make things happen for himself. This time it was in the form of Haltek, a huge electronics supply store in Mountain View. Haltek bought much of their inventory from the discontinued or excess parts sold off by the many local technical companies. Wireheads combed the store to find just the right piece or parts needed to create their own electronic devices. (Bill Fernandez and Woz were frequent customers who searched the store's bins and aisles.) For anyone into electronics, Haltek must have been like the best toy and candy stores wrapped into one and under one roof.

Steve loved spending time there. "Over time, Steve came to learn what all the parts were used for, how much they cost, and how to recognize good quality." On his own time, he would buy parts for a low price and sell them for a higher one, which echoed his own father's passion for fixing up old cars, then selling them for a profit.

In Steve's determined way, he convinced the people managing Haltek that they should hire him to work on weekends, which he did, starting in his sophomore year. Bill was now helping Woz build a computer (they called it the "Cream Soda Computer" because they drank Craigmont cream soda while they worked on it), so they made frequent trips to Haltek.

Steve was intrigued, not only by the computer Woz was building but also by Woz himself. "He was the first person I met who knew more electronics than I did."

Besides their passion for electronics, the two Steves had a lot in common. Both were considered outsiders. They were extremely bright and interested in subjects that many people didn't have the patience to understand. They both liked music. Steve was a Beatles fan. And thanks to Woz, he came to share Woz's passion for anything relating to Bob Dylan— his lyrics, his songs, his unique singing style, and his way of thinking: "Steve and I were into listening to

Bob Dylan and his lyrics, trying to figure out who was better, Dylan or the Beatles. We both favored Dylan because the songs were about life and living and values in life and what was really important. . . . To us, Dylan's songs struck a moral chord." And best of all, Steve discovered that Woz had the same inclination to be a serious prankster.

When Woz was about ten or eleven, he figured out how to connect his house to his friend's nearby with an intercom system created with simple wiring and switches. Without either set of parents knowing, the boys could call each other up and plan late-night activities. They'd sneak out of their bedroom windows to ride their bikes or even decorate a neighborhood girl's house with toilet paper.

One prank landed Woz in the custody of the police. He had built a metronome, a device that marks time with an adjustable regular ticking noise. It allows musicians to keep time with the music. But Woz realized it sounded like a ticking *bomb*. He took it to school and placed it inside the locker of a boy whose combination he knew. When a teacher heard the ticking, he opened the locker and bravely ran out to the football field, where he "disarmed" what he thought was a deadly device. The police were called, and Woz spent one night in juvenile detention. Woz's aptitude and talent for pranks made Steve feel that he'd met a like-minded person.

In 1971 Woz read an article in *Esquire* magazine, "Secrets of the Little Blue Box." It discussed the current fad among some electronic wizards, who were creating and using an electronic device to "trick" the phone company into making free long-distance calls. This brand of techies were called "phone phreaks." Today's computer hackers and phone phreaks require similar traits—a willingness to take risks (hacking and phone phreaking are both illegal), and expert technical skills.

Woz's earlier intercom wiring was similar to telephone wiring. When he read the article, he realized he wasn't alone in seriously fooling around with electronics. "These people were able to figure out that . . . they could make telephone calls within the Bell phone system for free."

Woz was fired up. He told Steve about the article, and they headed to the Stanford University library, where they found a manual detailing exactly how the phone system worked. After careful planning, Woz began to build a Blue Box. For years he had been designing and drawing prototypes of devices he wished he could build. Now was his chance.

When Woz told Steve about his plan to build a Blue Box, Steve realized they could sell the devices—something that had never occurred to Woz. Woz simply wanted to build his own Blue Box and have fun making free calls (mainly to Dial-a-Joke lines) around the world.

Once, Woz *really* expanded his reach and actually called the Vatican in Rome. Pretending to be then Secretary of State Henry Kissinger, he used a phony accent (Kissinger was born in Germany) and asked to speak to the pope. The pope was sleeping, but Woz requested a return call when he awoke!

Steve kept telling Woz of the financial potential of these Blue Boxes. He encouraged Woz to make more of them so they could create a business and sell them. They knew the device cheated the phone company and was illegal, but they went ahead anyway. It was risky, but they hoped their prior pranks would give them the skills they needed to avoid detection.

At the time, Woz was attending the University of California, Berkeley, about forty miles from Los Altos. Steve's car—paid for by earnings saved from Haltek—was essential for getting the two together. They spent hours in Woz's dorm room designing these boxes. They also concocted what they felt was a surefire plan to sell the illegal devices: "We'd knock on a [dorm room] door . . . and ask for someone nonexistent." They claimed that person had wanted a Blue Box. Then they'd describe what the Blue Box could do, and if the student didn't express any interest, they'd leave. But if the student did show an interest, the two Steves knew they had a possible customer— and most likely someone who wouldn't rat them out.

As for the pricing, that's where Steve's skills at Haltek came in. They bought parts at the lowest possible price and could assemble a box for forty dollars. Steve decided that the price should be one hundred fifty dollars. Over the next year, they actually made some money. But one time, when Steve's car broke down and the police pulled over to help them, the Blue Box posed a real problem. The police questioned them, and the two Steves talked themselves out of a possibly serious legal situation, convincing the police that the Blue Box was actually an electronic music synthesizer. That incident, coupled with a few more risky deals, brought this particular business partnership to an end.

Selling Blue Boxes wasn't Steve's only interest. He was spending less and less time attending Homestead and taking classes at nearby Stanford University. And he had a girlfriend, Chrisann.

When his car worked, he'd drive to the fully flowered "hippie" section in nearby San Francisco to hear the Beat poets. Steve, like Woz and many other young men at this time, had long hair. He wore torn blue jeans that Chrisann described as having more rips than pants.

A book from that time that held deep meaning for Steve was *The Whole Earth Catalog*, which complemented and expanded Steve's own philoso-phies. Originally published in 1968, the catalog's creator, Stewart Brand, believed that people needed to take control of their own lives, their own educa-tion, and their environment. But instead of living a far simpler life, Brand felt people should embrace mod-ern technology, especially computers. The informa-tion he provided was far-ranging, from his personal philosophy to discussions of well-made products that would simplify and empower people's lives.

In 1972 Steve was ready for college. If he chose one of the state colleges or universities close to home, it would have meant less of a financial burden for Paul and Clara. However, he had known some older kids who attended Reed, an expensive liberal arts college in Portland, Oregon, more than six hun-dred miles away. After a visit to the school, he had decided that Reed was the only college he wanted to go to. The financial obligation on his parents had to have been enormous—but Paula and Clara had made a commitment seventeen years ago. Steve was prepared to leave California and Chrisann behind.

The family piled into the car and drove the almost twelve-hour trip to Reed College—Steve's new base.

When Steve left for college, he joined many people his age who used those years to explore: new ways of thinking, new ways of living, new ways of viewing the world and their place in it. The only problem? He wasn't doing that exploring in his scheduled classes. His grades were poor, and his parents were very upset with him. They urged him to apply himself, but instead, right before Christmas . . .

"After six months, I couldn't see the value in it. I had no idea what I wanted to do with my life and no idea how college was going to help me figure it out. And here I was spending all of the money my parents had saved their entire life. So I decided to drop out and trust that it would all work out okay. It was pretty scary at the time."

However, he didn't leave Portland or Reed. He was determined to let his education continue—in any way possible. He'd made two strong friendships at Reed: Dan Kottke and an older student, Robert

PATRICIA LAKIN

Friedland. Instead of renting a dorm room or a local apartment, Steve either camped out in his friends' dorms or found empty dorm rooms that had been vacated by other dropouts. When he'd exhausted the free sleeping arrangements, Steve worked odd jobs so he could rent a cheap room close to Reed's campus.

Now all he needed was money for food. Food and diet were other areas Steve explored. He read many books on different theories of diets and how each affected one's body. He was eager to experiment with whichever diet he was studying at the time. He stuck to very specific foods—like eating a diet only of fruit. On some occasions, he decided to fast and not eat for hours, or even for days—all as a way, in his mind, to find a better, healthier lifestyle.

Steve subscribed to the belief that if he ate very specific foods, he wouldn't sweat or have body odor. No body odor meant he could eliminate the need to shower. It wasn't a theory that worked: His body odor was evident to Dan's girlfriend, Elizabeth Holmes.

Body odor or not, he and Dan became close

friends. They were both bright, considered outsiders in their hometowns, and they were exploring life's meaning together. Since money was tight for Steve, he and Dan would walk or get a ride to a totally different section of Portland on Sunday nights, seven miles from Reed. There, at a Hare Krishna temple, any and all comers were served free and strictly vegetarian dishes. When he wasn't fasting, or eating at the temple, Steve's diet consisted of oatmeal and milk from the Reed cafeteria. It was around this time that Steve became a vegetarian, a diet he was to follow for the rest of his life.

Steve and Dan were both close friends of Robert Friedland, who walked around campus wearing a style of dress more commonly seen in India—long, draping cloth robes. He spoke often of his trip to India, his studies of Zen Buddhism, his Indian guru (or spiritual teacher), and how it all influenced his life. Robert's experiences, conversations, and ideas lit a fire for Steve and Dan. India had to be their next destination.

4

CALLIGRAPHY +
ZEN BUDDHISM + ATARI

STEVE'S INTERESTS AT REED AND IN Portland were varied and widespread. Diets, Zen Buddhism, and traveling to India were not all that he thought about: "Throughout the [Reed College] campus every poster, every label on every drawer was beautifully hand-calligraphed. Because I had dropped out and didn't have to take the normal classes, I decided to take a calligraphy class to learn how to do this."

The word "calligraphy" (from Greek) combines two words: "beauty" and "write." It is the art of writing by hand with pen or brush in a beautiful and distinctive style.

The calligraphy program at Reed was started in 1949 by Lloyd Reynolds, a freethinking, philosophical, self-taught, highly popular professor. In his calligraphy class, Reynolds constantly made connections between the art of beautiful writing and the works of great artists like Michelangelo; he also related calligraphy to the beliefs of Zen Buddhism.

When Steve dropped in on this course, Reynolds had already taken a leave of absence from Reed. However, he'd carefully selected his replacement: a talented, like-minded calligraphy teacher, Friar Robert Palladino. This former monk, who had once taken an eighteen-year vow of silence, was Steve's teacher. Palladino described his teaching style: "We would concentrate on one style of writing at a time. I would lecture not only on that particular style of writing, but what was going on in the world at that time that conditioned the kind of art that evolved. All those things are very important." Palladino also gave his definition of his cherished art. "Calligraphy is graphic music moving with rhythmic gesture across a field of silent space which surrounds it."

In the class, Steve "learned about serif and sans serif typefaces, about varying the amount of space between different letter combinations, about what makes great typography great. It was beautiful, historical, artistically subtle in a way that science can't capture, and I found it fascinating."

It's no wonder that this inspired instructor with his spiritual linking of life and letters made a strong impression on Steve. The concept of beautiful details making graphic music was the kind of nonconformist or "outside the box" thinking that captured Steve's imagination.

This class proved to be a significant experience for Steve. Remember, he had been taught by his father to pay close attention to the tiniest of details, as it was those very details that made one's creation something truly valuable. The beauty of lettering with swirls, lines, and perfectly planned spacing spoke to Steve in a very profound way (and today can be seen in the lettering on Apple's signs, ads, products, and packaging).

Besides the classes Steve audited, his friendships with Dan and Robert continued to be meaningful influences as well. Friedland was often found on a relative's thirty-five-acre farm in nearby rural Oregon. Named the All-One Farm, it had a large apple orchard. Friedland helped to maintain the farm with a group of friends. Steve and Dan visited frequently and would pitch in, tending to the orchard on the property.

When not working the farm, they listened to Friedland sing the praises of his guru, Neem Karoli Baba, and of India. Friedland boasted that with the teachings of this guru and a trip to India, one could find the answers to the meaning of life. Steve felt that if he wanted to learn and discover more about himself, including his spiritual side, he would need to travel to India. Dan felt this same pull as well. Steve and Dan now had a common goal, but it was a goal that would have to wait: Neither one had the money to travel halfway around the world.

Steve continued to drop in only on the classes that interested him (even a modern dance class, whose choreographed moves he felt compared to the movement of objects in computer video games). But he was getting tired of finding places to sleep and food to eat, and scraping by with very limited money. After eighteen months of living hand to mouth, he decided to head home and live with his parents. He knew he needed a job, especially because going to India was now his primary goal and a costly one.

Steve moved back home to Los Altos in 1974. In those days, the best place to hunt for a job was by looking through want ads in newspapers. One that caught his eye said, "Have fun and make money." What could be better? But would he get the job? That uncertainty never crossed his mind. When he showed up at the address listed, Steve was just as forward and persistent as he had been when he'd called Bill Hewlett years earlier. The office he entered was a two-year-old video game company called Atari. He was hired that same day.

The man who hired him, Al Alcorn, had developed the video game Pong, which was a huge success for Atari. Years later, Alcorn recalled the day

Steve applied. "One day the personnel director came by and said, 'We've got this weird guy here. He says he won't leave until we hire him. We either call the cops or we take him.'" Alcorn went on, "He [Steve] was determined to have the job, and there was some spark, some inner energy, an attitude that he was going to get it done." Alcorn assigned Steve to work with one particular employee, who complained, "What are you giving me this guy for? He has BO and he's different, a . . . hippie."

Alcorn sensed Steve's abilities and drive and wanted him to stay. Atari was a fast-growing company, and they needed a "hippie whiz kid" like Steve. He was asked to work at night with one other person. Steve worked hard and saved money for his trip. But then he thought, why not have Atari make the trip happen? Steve asked Alcorn to pay his way to India so Steve could see his guru. Alcorn thought the idea ridiculous, but he came up with a plan that would help them both: Technicians in Germany were having problems with Atari equipment that he thought Steve could fix. He agreed to send Steve to

Germany, where he'd work, earn some money, and then take a leave of absence to travel to India.

Steve accepted Alcorn's offer and called Dan Kottke. After Steve's work was done in Germany, the two planned to meet in India, where they'd first see Robert's guru and then explore the country together.

For many generations India had been a place to discover "inner peace." In the late 1960s and early 1970s, it was a popular destination for people seeking "enlightenment." They would often stay in ashrams, centers of spiritual learning that offered meditation, yoga, and other teachings—all paths to personal transformation. Adding to India's allure for westerners was the Beatles' pilgrimage to Rishikesh, in February of 1968, to study transcendental meditation with Maharishi Mahesh Yogi.

Steve arrived in New Delhi, India's capital, a few weeks ahead of Dan. In 1974 India had the second largest population in the world: six hundred million people. To understand just what Steve may have seen when he came to New Delhi that summer, picture a huge city at night—semidark streets, throngs of people, honking cars, bikes and scooters, all moving aside for the many wandering sacred cows that freely roamed the city.

For all its historical and cultural attractions, this capital city was also overcrowded—lacking enough jobs, homes, and food for its millions of residents. There were signs of poverty all over: in buildings that needed repair, in the garbage-strewn streets, and in the eyes of those who had no home at all. One could see it in their worn, threadbare clothing, their bare feet, and their outstretched hands, asking for some little bit of food to eat.

Steve had worn ripped jeans as a teenager and went barefoot by choice. He had gone for days without food by choice. Now he was witnessing many who wore torn clothing and no shoes and who went hungry because they had no choice.

While he waited for Dan's arrival, he decided to take a trip north of New Delhi, following the Ganges, India's most sacred river. This 1,569-mile-long river springs from the Himalayas, then ribbons its way south and empties into the Bay of Bengal in the east.

Hinduism is the dominant religion of India, and many of its followers regard the Ganges as sacred. Its waters are thought to rid people of any sins or sickness. It is a place to bath, to wash one's clothes, and also a place to seek comfort when ill or near death. Families bring their dead to this river.

As Steve walked along the Ganges's banks, he saw small, giggling children brushing their teeth or splashing joyfully, people his age beating clothes clean along the river's edge, and the sick and dying. The effect these observations had on him was profound. He was, after all, someone who thought deeply and carefully. Knowing that in the course of one minute, one easily sees all phases of life in India, his experiences must have been at the same time heartwarming, heart-wrenching, and heart-stopping.

One heart-wrenching experience came when Steve and Dan discovered that the very guru (Neem Karoli Baba) they had come so far to see had died the previous fall. Despite the disappointment, they found a spot in India where they stayed for a month: reading, thinking, meditating, and walking in the nearby villages. But it was summer, and summer in India is brutally hot.

Eventually they heard of another guru. Since meeting a guru had been their mission, they decided to walk the many miles to his village. The road was a narrow, rock-strewn, difficult path to climb. Their feet were rubbed raw, even though they wore sandals. Their cotton clothing didn't block out the sun's rays beating down on them. When they finally reached the guru, they found him uninspiring. His answers to their questions didn't show any thought, intelligence, or depth. As they left the guru's village, it grew dark and the skies opened up with a driving rain—they could see only when lightning lit up the sky. Scared, tired, and sick from dysentery, they knew it was time to leave India.

When recalling that trip, Steve said, "We weren't going to find a place where we could go for a month to be enlightened. It was one of the first times I started thinking that maybe Thomas Edison did a lot more to improve the world than Karl Marx and Neem Karoli Baba put together."

What did he mean? Thomas Edison is known for inventing the lightbulb and the phonograph, inventions that positively altered people's lives and well-being all over the world. Neem Karoli Baba was a spiritual teacher and thinker who imparted wisdom to his followers. Karl Marx, a German philosopher and intellectual, wrote about social and economic issues in the mid-1800s. Steve's point was that Edison actually "made" something as his way of contributing to the world. The other two men, important as they were, produced thoughts, not things.

After returning from India, Steve's quest for self-discovery continued closer to home. The tenets and practices of Hinduism (including karma) and Zen Buddhism (seeking enlightenment through meditation, which he had already been doing in Portland and in India) influenced his thinking more than ever. He decided to find his own guru.

While searching, Steve bounced between California and the All-One Farm in Oregon. At the farm, he rigged up a vast electrical system in one of the barns to

Steve Jobs: Thinking Differently

create a workplace where they could make and then sell wood-burning stoves, a style of stove recommended in the 1971 *Whole Earth Catalog*. When Robert saw what Steve had accomplished, he was amazed; he hadn't realized that Steve was capable of this sort of technical work. They were close friends, and yet Steve had never shared his expertise in and passion for electronics with Robert.

In California, Steve found a Zen teacher and center right in Los Altos. Kobun Chino Otogawa was in charge at the Haiku Zen Center. Steve began spending more and more time with Kobun, both at the center and at Kobun's house. He also accompanied Kobun on meditation retreats at a Zen Buddhist monastery in California—Kobun was the teacher, and Steve drank in the knowledge that he offered.

For the rest of his life, Steve felt meditating was of utmost importance. Through the practice of meditation—once he soothed his fast-thinking mind and his ever-moving body—he found he was able to achieve an inner sense of calm. It was then that he felt he could notice things more clearly. Essential

PATRICIA LAKIN

inner truths and paths he should choose in life were finally able to emerge.

Two major issues surfaced for Steve at this time. The first, since he was still trying to discover just who he was, focused on finding who his biological parents were. His own personality quirks could be explained if he knew more about them. But then, not wanting to appear disloyal to his parents, Paul and Clara, he dismissed the idea of tracking them down.

The second was when Steve asked Kobun Chino Otogawa whether he should go to Japan and enter a monastery. Kobun advised Steve that he could be in touch with his spirituality *and* still work in the business world. Had Kobun Chino Otogawa picked up on Steve's great desire to create something new as Edison had done? What did Steve want to create?

5

SEEDS OF APPLE

TEVE WAS TWENTY YEARS OLD AT the start of 1975. Whatever creative path he planned to take, he knew he needed a job. He returned to one place where he'd worked before—Atari.

As someone who always operated on his own terms, Steve headed to Atari's offices dressed as *he* chose. It never occurred to him to comb his hair, put on shoes, and wear a clean shirt. He entered the offices dressed as if he were an Indian wise man, barefoot and in a flowing orange robe. They welcomed Steve back, not surprised by his attire.

Steve also reconnected with Woz, who since 1973 had been working at Hewlett-Packard, his dream job as an engineer now a reality. While Steve had been off in India, Woz also continued doing what he loved: designing various electronic projects and trying to build his own computer. He'd figured out a way to hook up an inexpensive TV to his computer to serve as a monitor. He also attached a cheap type-writer keyboard so that information could be easily entered. Woz's main objective: build an *affordable* computer with a minimum number of parts but one that could do a maximum number of things. With other computers of that era, the only way to enter data was to use the front panel of switches, turning them off or on in a particular pattern. It was a considerable nuisance.

While Woz was immersed in Hewlett-Packard and his after-hours interests, Steve approached him to do freelance work at Atari. Steve was working on a new video game called Breakout, which Atari's founder, Nolan Bushnell, had designed. It was like

Pong, but it required the player to "break out" of a brick wall.

Woz agreed to help, but since he was employed at Hewlett-Packard during the day, he toiled alongside Steve at night. Added to that pressure was that they had only *four days* to complete the project and had to use as few silicon chips as possible. Woz worked tirelessly designing, while Steve concentrated on wiring and installing the chips needed for the game. (They finished the job, but Woz recalled, "Steve and I both ended up with mononucleosis.") As they worked, they talked: Steve told Woz that Atari wanted to eventually use the newly created microprocessors in their video games.

In 1974 the computer world was overflowing with new developments and breakthroughs that would forever change the landscape. One of the most significant came in the summer of 1974, when Intel's creation of the microprocessor was announced. Microprocessors allowed computers to grow in speed and capability but shrink in size. This small and powerful chip was "command central" for a computer. And it meant home computing was more of a possibility than ever before.

Woz wasn't 100 percent sure what microprocessors were capable of. But he did know that a microprocessor was like having a tiny computer *inside* a game—and the potential capabilities of this excited and inspired him.

The rest of the world was not particularly interested in the world of computers. The average person didn't know—and didn't care—that any of this was happening. Even the companies that made the tremendous mainframe computers firmly believed that business and industry were the only markets for these smaller machines and doubted that people would actually ever want a computer in their home.

But the wireheads living in Silicon Valley believed otherwise.

With all the recent technological advances, a group of California-based computer enthusiasts formed a club to share and trade ideas with other hobbyists and engineers who dreamed of building their own computers. They called themselves the Homebrew Computer Club and had their first meeting in March 1975 at the Menlo Park garage of Gordon French.

What started with thirty members soon grew to several hundred attendees, who now met at the auditorium of the Stanford Linear Accelerator Center in Menlo Park.

Some hobbyists were simply interested in the field and the new developments. At meetings, they discussed the newly formed companies that were actually making home computers (these machines didn't have many functions, unless they were add-ons purchased separately), which were still too expensive for the average person.

Steve wasn't as initially enthralled as Woz was with Homebrew. From the start, Woz fit in and shared the same goals: "We thought low-cost computers would empower people to do things they never could before. . . . In this, we were revolutionaries. . . . How people lived and communicated was going to be changed by us, changed forever, changed more than anyone could predict exactly. . . . As I said, almost all of the large computer companies were on record saying that what we were doing was insignificant.

PATRICIA LAKIN

It turned out they were wrong and we were right—right all the way. But back then, even we had no idea how right we were and how huge it would become."

Two months earlier, in January 1975, a home computer called Altair had been introduced.

Jobs said of the event, "It was so amazing to all of us that somebody had actually come up with a way to build a computer you could own yourself. That had never been possible. . . . But now, for the first time, you could actually buy a computer. The Altair was a kit that came out around 1975 and sold for less than four hundred dollars."

People could buy the computer assembled or in a kit. While the company sold far more than they ever imagined, even the Homebrew members felt that the Altair left a lot to be desired. The Altair was a computer in a metal box. On the front were switches and lights. Monitor? Keyboard? Memory capabilities? These small computers had none of those features.

However, all these computer breakthroughs gave Steve an idea for the path he wanted to take. All he had to do was convince Woz. Why Woz? For Steve,

Woz was a logical and clever choice to be his partner. Both Steves had the same goal—creating an inexpensive computer for the average person. And Steve thought of people like Woz, the ever-growing members of the Homebrew Computer Club, and devoted *Whole Earth Catalog* readers. He saw a way to give all of them exactly what they wanted.

Steve also realized that these techies had little time or money to design and build their own computers. But if they could buy a *predesigned* and printed circuit board—the board that held all the internal components of a computer—they could eliminate a time-consuming first step.

Woz's beautifully designed circuit boards would be an easy sell.

Steve knew that Woz was a perfectionist who slaved over making the labor-intensive wire circuitry on his boards as compact and as efficient as possible. He soldered the wires instead of wire-wrapping his boards so that no unsightly wires stuck out. Going into business to print and sell Woz's circuit boards had to be the next right step.

During January and February of 1976, Steve kept talking to Woz about the idea of starting a business. He assured Woz that he could still work at his beloved Hewlett-Packard, and Steve would continue to come and go at Atari. He told Woz that they could do this business on the side. The very shy Woz was concerned about selling the product himself, but Steve would make the necessary phone and sales calls and they'd split the profits fifty-fifty.

One day, as they zipped along Route 85 in Steve's VW van, Steve knew just how to approach his friend. "I can remember him [Steve] saying this like it was yesterday," Woz recalled. "'Well, even if we lose our money, we'll have a company. For once in our lives, we'll have a company.' That convinced me. And I was excited to think about us like that. To be two best friends starting a company. Wow."

Later, Woz asked Steve what they should call their business.

"Apple," popped out of Steve's mouth.

Steve Jobs: Thinking Differently

6

THE MOM-AND-POP COMPUTER SHOP

PPLE? APPLE COMPUTER? WHAT kind of name was that for a company? Woz kept trying to think up more technical-sounding names, like Executek and Matrix. But Steve said, "If we can't think of anything else, we'll stick with Apple."

Stick with Apple they did. But why "Apple"? Was Steve trusting his gut, sensing that Apple was just a quirky or unconventional enough name to be perfect?

For Steve, there were two obvious "apple" associations: He'd worked on the All-One Farm tending

PATRICIA LAKIN

to their apple orchard. And he often consumed an all-fruit diet.

Neither of the Steves knew about business plans or contracts, but they knew they needed money to get started. Steve calculated that buying the boards and printing them would cost them about twenty-five dollars each. If they made one hundred boards, they'd need $2,500. They agreed to split this initial cost, but neither had much money.

Woz was earning a decent salary at Hewlett-Packard but was spending it on everything from stereo equipment to computer parts to his upcoming marriage. Steve's only item of value was his VW van. His dad hadn't thought it was worth much when his son first purchased it, but Steve could sell it for $1,500. Woz sold his cherished Hewlett-Packard 65 calculator, hoping to get $500 but winding up with $250.

Unfortunately, Steve's van was returned when it broke down. He agreed to pay for half the repair, but that took a huge chunk out of his savings. Somehow, the Steves scraped together what they needed and found someone who would print up Woz's circuit boards.

Steve also convinced Woz to include one other partner, forty-one-year-old Ron Wayne, who had come to work at Atari after his Nevada business failed. Since Woz knew that he and Steve were not the most business savvy, he agreed to include Wayne. It was decided that for Wayne's expertise, he would own 10 percent of the company. Woz and Steve divided the rest equally, at 45 percent each.

Wayne volunteered to draft a contract, write the initial operating manual, and draw their logo, which depicted Sir Isaac Newton (the scientist who formulated the law of gravity) sitting under an apple tree.

On April Fool's Day in 1976, when Steve was just twenty-one years old, the three gathered to sign the contract in Wayne's Mountain View apartment. Steve was the only one to pen his name in all lowercase letters.

But it didn't take long for Ron to become nervous, given his prior experience. Since the agreement was a partnership, any debts caused by one partner would have to be shared equally. Wayne had strong doubts that the money Steve urgently wanted to spend now for Apple Computer could ever be earned back, and he feared he could soon find himself deeply in debt. So, eleven days later, he filed the necessary papers to withdraw from the agreement. He received money for his time, the writing of the legal agreement, and the drawing. Once again, the two Steves were fifty-fifty partners. (It's been calculated that had Ron Wayne kept his 10 percent share, he'd now be a billionaire.)

Steve and Woz proceeded to make up a circuit board to show at the Homebrew Computer Club. At the club's weekly gathering, while Woz discussed his design, Steve identified members more interested in the business end of computers than the building of them. Paul Terrell, a Homebrew regular, was one such man. After the Altair and other minicomputers came out, Terrell wanted to sell home computers and had already opened up a computer shop, the Byte Shop. He, like Steve, felt that home computers could be a booming business. His first store was located in Mountain View, on El Camino Real, a long, busy thoroughfare.

When Steve approached him at Homebrew,

Terrell wasn't impressed with him or his appearance. He gave Steve his business card anyway and said, "Keep in touch."

The very next day, carrying a completed circuit board, a barefoot Steve waltzed into Byte. "I'm keeping in touch," he announced. Terrell hoped that Steve and Woz actually had a *finished* computer, not just a simple circuit board with a few chips and no microprocessor—the "brains" in the computer. He told Steve exactly what he had been expecting—a fully assembled, fully built, functioning computer.

A good negotiator, Steve asked Terrell how much he'd be willing to pay. Terrell responded that he'd pay five hundred dollars each, cash on delivery, for fifty Apple computers.

Steve later recalled that as he heard Terrell's words, all he could see were dollar signs dancing before his eyes. He agreed to Terrell's offer, rushed out of the store, and immediately called Woz at work. "I was shocked, just completely shocked," Woz said. "It was the first and most astounding success for Apple the company."

PATRICIA LAKIN

Steve Jobs: Thinking Differently

But now they really needed serious funding in order to purchase parts and fill the order. There was no question that fast-talking Steve, not shy Woz, was the person for the job.

Once again, Steve operated completely his own way. That he didn't shower often, had uncombed hair, and often went barefoot didn't seem to be important to him. This was who he was, and if he had an interview with a business executive, how he dressed shouldn't be of any importance. He soon learned that it was.

Steve approached Nolan Bushnell, the founder of Atari, who invited one of his major investors to meet with Steve. That man couldn't see past Steve's unkempt look. And during the meeting, when Steve put his bare feet on the man's desk, Bushnell knew there wouldn't be a deal to invest in Steve or Apple Computer.

After a series of nos from a local bank and other businessmen, including the owner of Haltek (Steve's former place of work), he approached another electronics supply house, Cramer Electronics. The person in charge couldn't believe that the disheveled, barefoot kid was serious. Could he really have an order for fifty computers that he was selling to Terrell? Steve insisted that Terrell should be called immediately. Terrell was at a conference, but he was paged over the loudspeaker and told he had an emergency call. Much to the disbelief of the employee at Cramer, Terrell came to the phone and confirmed Steve's account. In turn, Cramer approved the order: thirty days in which to pay the bill for the computer parts, *without* having to pay any interest, which would cut into their profits.

Apple Computer went into high gear—they had to create fifty computers from scratch. *Fifty* computers in *thirty* days. This do-it-yourself fledgling company started assembling the Byte Shop order in Woz's apartment, his kitchen table converted into a storage area with an array of parts and a big sign warning not to touch one thing. Ann, his new wife, wasn't too pleased with this arrangement, so Apple decided to move their operation to Steve's house—his parents' house—in Los Altos.

Starting in Patty's old bedroom, the work then spread and expanded to the rest of the house, eventually moving into the garage, which Paul Jobs rearranged. Everyone got into the act: Patty, now expecting her first child, put chips carefully into place on the circuit board. Steve's friend Dan Kottke and his girlfriend, Elizabeth, lived nearby. Elizabeth was in charge of soldering, but when she botched a few attempts, Steve blew up at her, put her on the accounting detail, and took over the soldering himself.

There was no office and no staff. Believing that Apple Computer should sound like a professional business, Steve had hired an answering service. Messages were directed to the house, where Steve's mom would either write them down or call them out to announce whatever the prospective buyer's question was.

Out in the garage, Woz was testing each finished circuit board. If they worked, he placed them in one box. If there was a glitch, he labored over the workbench and tried to discover the problem. Paul Jobs rigged up a device that would test the computers when they were on. He'd leave them on overnight to make sure the computers weren't overheating.

When the first few computers were finished, Steve carefully loaded up the car and drove to the Byte Shop. When Terrell saw what he'd purchased, he wasn't pleased. He told Steve that he'd ordered *fully functioning* computers. These had no keyboard, no power cord, and no case. What Steve had presented to him were just glorified circuit boards. But Steve stood firm, and somewhat amazingly, Terrell honored his agreement.

But now they went back to work and had to give Terrell what he wanted. The computers Woz had already built could easily be hooked up to a keyboard. He also knew how to connect the computer to a monitor. Neither task was a problem. They selected a power cord and got busy.

A fully functioning computer also needed software, or a language, that could direct the computer to perform additional functions. Woz had some knowledge of BASIC, a common language then being used. Some members of the Homebrew Computer

Club bought a copy of BASIC and made free copies that they traded. Sharing was key. (At the time, one software developer was furious that a language he'd developed was being passed around for free. He complained in a letter to the Homebrew members, asking how they expected new software to be developed if the developers' products were being ripped off. The letter was signed "Bill Gates." Despite Gates's plea, Woz worked on mastering BASIC to upload into their latest computer.)

At the time, there wasn't yet a way for a computer to "remember" or hold data in its memory (including the BASIC software that had been entered). When the computer was shut off, *poof!*—the entered language was gone. Woz came up with an ingenious solution. He entered the BASIC language onto a cassette tape. When the computer was turned on, the cassette was inserted into a special slot, and the language would upload quickly. This revolutionary approach meant that the user wouldn't have to memorize pages and pages of a code and enter it each time the computer was turned on.

Finally the official Apple I computers were delivered to the Byte Shop—but with no cases. Terrell took them anyway and hired a cabinetmaker to create wooden cases. Steve, Woz, and Terrell had already established the computer's retail price at $666.66.

Now they had to wait and see—would the Apple I computer actually sell?

7

BRING IN THE SUITS

N THE SUMMER OF 1976 TWO HISTORIC events were celebrated in the United States: the nation's bicentennial and the landing of the *Viking 1* spacecraft on Mars. Perhaps not momentous to the rest of the country was that Paul and Clara Jobs were pretty tired of living among a houseful of round-the-clock workers, scattered electrical parts, and half-eaten food lying about. Paul's solution was to take his cars out of the garage, leave them parked on the street, and turn the entire garage over to Steve and Woz. As he reasoned, his cars wouldn't be damaged if they were outside, but the computer equipment would.

True to Paul's nature, he made sure Steve's new business workplace would be neat and organized. He put up shelves, clearly labeled and stored the electrical parts on the shelves, and installed a long workbench so that computers could easily be assembled.

Steve and Woz had delivered the promised fifty Apple computers to Terrell's Byte Shop. The plan now was to build fifty more, which Steve would try to sell at other computer shops that were springing up around Silicon Valley.

The two Steves were immersed in their new business, working day and night, seven days a week. Woz was still at HP, but all his spare time was spent at Steve's house. Steve wasn't married and didn't have a full-time commitment with Atari, so he wasn't under the same kind of pressure as Woz. But he worried that their new business might mushroom, be all-consuming, and not allow him the time to pursue his spiritual side. Exploring the "nature of things" was just as important to Steve as his business life. He consulted with Kobun Chino Otogawa and told him he was seriously considering going to Japan to enter a monastery. If he chose to go to Japan, he thought, he might never return. But Kobun had assured Steve that being in business was the same as sitting in a monastery.

What made Steve's Zen master believe that two such different paths in life could yield the same results? Kobun probably knew Steve far better than Steve knew himself and understood how intense a person he was. Whatever Steve chose, monk or businessman, he would constantly strive for perfection and would devote his waking hours to achieving just that—perfection.

But Steve was still not sure. To sort things out, he took long walks either alone or with friends. On one particular walk, he turned to his high school buddy Bill Fernandez and confided that of all the businessmen he knew, he didn't like any of them and certainly didn't want to turn into one.

Woz was experiencing his own turmoil, but not the spiritual kind. His stress was computer related. He thought the Apple I was a terrific machine but was primarily built in a patched-together way to fit Terrell's specifications. It reflected work he had done from computers he'd built in the *past*. Now there was new equipment, and he had new and different ideas he was itching to try. He'd been longing to start on a brand-new computer he could build from the ground up. During that summer he began to carve out time to work on what he called the Apple II.

Despite the various pressures Steve and Woz faced, the two partners boarded a plane and headed to Atlantic City just before Labor Day. This seaside resort in New Jersey was the location of PC '76, an annual computer festival. The Apple I rested carefully on Steve's lap, and the still-primitive Apple II sat on the fold-down tray so Woz could tend to it. Other Homebrew Club Members, some of whom had been creating their own computers, were also on the flight. Two sat behind them and leaned forward to examine the Apple II prototype. Acting like childish bullies, they declared Steve and Woz's computer thoroughly unimpressive. As Woz remembered it, besides their snide comment, they talked in a business lingo that Woz said sounded like a foreign language. He felt like he was out of his league with this group.

No such thought ever entered Steve's mind. After they arrived in Atlantic City and set up their booth, Steve took time to observe what the other exhibitors had to show. As he strolled among the other displays, Steve realized Paul Terrell had been right: A computer had to have fully integrated parts—that meant a built-in keyboard and a monitor. All the user should have to do was plug in the computer and voilà—everything would be ready to go. Steve thought if an all-in-one type of computer were to be sold, the market would reach far beyond the hobbyists to millions of everyday consumers.

One night in their hotel room, while still at the convention, Woz took out the Apple II prototype. He desperately wanted to create a computer monitor with a full-color display, his dream ever since he and Steve had worked on Breakout for Atari. He was able to successfully connect the Apple II to a color TV. But could this computer be hooked up to and work with other projection devices? That was Woz's concern.

The two Steves asked a projectionist assigned to the convention to have a projector accessible. Woz connected the Apple II and the projector, and it displayed the color perfectly. Woz and Steve were overjoyed. Projecting data in color for large groups could be an exceptional selling point for the Apple II. And the projectionist, who'd seen the wide array of computers on display, told them that of all the computers at the conference, theirs was the only one he'd buy.

Of course, this computer was not yet for sale. With Steve's realization that a fully integrated computer was way to go, the two returned to California determined to create the best computer possible— the Apple II.

Woz thought they'd reached their goal when he'd been able to program and play Breakout on their Apple II prototype. With video games now being sold as software, Woz was sure the Apple II would be a surefire hit with all the gamers—and viewed in living color! He said, "I designed the Apple II so it

PATRICIA LAKIN

Steve Jobs: Thinking Differently

would work with the color TV you already owned. And it had game control paddles you could attach to it, and sound built in. That made it the first computer people wanted to design arcade-style games for, the first computer with sound and paddles ready to go."

But Steve had further requirements and refinements for the Apple II. They needed a specially designed, beautiful plastic case to house their new computer. Steve knew that hiring a designer (Jerry Manock) would be expensive. Also, he wanted a computer without the noisy cooling fan, essential so that heat wouldn't build up. Steve was insistent that they find an engineer who could create a power supply device that wouldn't overheat, thus eliminating the need for a fan. He said, "The real jump with the Apple II was that it was a finished product. It was the first computer that you could buy that wasn't a kit. It was fully assembled and had its own case and its own keyboard and you could really sit down and start to use it."

Steve asked Al Alcorn, who knew about electrical

engineering, and he recommended Rod Holt. He took one look at these longhaired guys working away in a garage and warned them, "I'm expensive." They assured Holt they could pay. Holt decided to take the job because it was an intriguing challenge, as this kind of device didn't exist yet. He wound up spending a fair amount of time with Steve and Woz even when he wasn't working on his assignment.

To produce the Apple II, Steve knew they needed funds now more than ever. He approached one of the richest men he knew, Nolan Bushnell, and asked if he'd be willing to put up $50,000 in exchange for one-third of Apple Computer. Bushnell later said that he thought himself so smart that he rejected Steve's offer. He went on to add that he laughs about it now when he's not crying.

Steve, ever persistent, then asked Bushnell if he knew anyone who *would* be interested in investing in Apple Computer. It was through Bushnell that Steve was put in touch with Mike Markkula, a thirty-three-year-old retired multimillionaire. He had been an electrical engineer at Intel and cashed in the valuable

Intel stocks he'd owned. Markkula would provide the critical business experience Apple Computer needed. At his first meeting with Steve and Woz, Markkula suggested they write up a business plan, the usual first step when starting a company. Markkula agreed to invest if he liked their business plan. It turned out that Markkula wound up writing the plan, investing $250,000 ($80,000 as an investment; $170,000 as a loan), and becoming a partner in the company.

Markkula's investment came with certain conditions: Woz had to quit his job at HP. There was no way that he could put in the hours of work necessary to develop Apple Computer and hold down another job.

This made sense to everyone but Woz. He loved his job as an engineer at HP and couldn't think of ever giving it up. He thought long and hard and told Steve and Markkula no. Steve was beside himself. He did what he had done since he was a little kid—he cried. He rushed over to Woz's house and cried and begged for Woz to reconsider. When that didn't work, Steve called Jerry Wozniak and other mutual friends to pressure Woz to change his mind. It was their high

Steve Jobs: Thinking Differently

PATRICIA LAKIN   79

school friend Allen Baum who saved the day. As Woz later recalled, "He told me he thought it was absolutely possible for me to start a company and stay an engineer." And Woz went on, "I needed to hear one person saying that I could stay at the bottom of the organization chart, as an engineer, and not have to be a manager." Allen's honest and logical argument did the trick. Woz went to Steve and Mike and told them he'd quit HP. Now it was full steam ahead to get the Apple II up and running and sold.

Mike Markkula strongly believed this new company could soon become one of the five hundred biggest companies and had very definite ideas on how to get Apple Computer to reach that goal. He imparted his three-point business philosophy to Steve. First, a business needed to show *empathy* for its customers by answering their needs better than any other company. Second was *focus*: "In order to do a good job of those things that we decide to do, we must eliminate all of the unnecessary opportunities." And third was *impute*, which to Markkula's thinking simply meant that how a company presents itself and its products *imputes* or gives

PATRICIA LAKIN

an impression of that company to its customers. Mike shared his belief that people *do* judge books by their covers. If something is attractive on the outside and also proves to be a good product, there's a strong chance that it will be a hit. In Mike's view, if the product is great but the design or packaging isn't as worthy, people view the product and possibly the company negatively.

That last word, "impute," was something Steve might never have verbalized. But long ago and deep down, he had embraced the importance of *impute* as well. Steve's dad had instilled in him a pride in craftsmanship—from the inside out. Steve's appreciation of calligraphy and typefaces spoke to his profound sense of the beauty and spacing of letters as well as to the power of the written word. His spiritual belief, Zen Buddhism, celebrated nature in its simplest, purest forms. As for *focus* and *empathy*, Steve had faith in Markkula and listened carefully to that advice. Instinctively, though, he already knew about customer *empathy*—that was why he had been adamant that the Apple I be a machine that customers could use with ease.

Keeping Markkula's points in mind, Steve noticed that Intel's advertisements were distinctive in their design and simplicity. He called Intel and asked what advertising agency was responsible. He was directed to Regis McKenna, an agency located in Palo Alto, named for the man who founded it. Steve contacted them immediately and was directed to an assistant, Frank Burge. Steve told Burge, "You guys do good stuff; I'd like you to do mine." Burge said he'd pass on the message and call back.

No call came. Steve called daily and left messages. Finally Burge agreed to come out to Apple Computer's headquarters—the Jobs family's garage.

Burge later recalled thinking, "What's the least amount of time I can spend with this clown without being rude and then get back to something more profitable." After scruffy-haired and unbathed Steve greeted him, Burge soon realized two things: "First, he was an incredibly smart young man. Second, I didn't understand a fiftieth of what he was talking about."

Luckily for Steve, Burge was able to check Steve's references with a current Regis McKenna client, Paul

Terrell, whose Byte Shops were popping up all over the area. Terrell vouched for Steve, and an appointment was scheduled at the agency.

Markkula, Woz, and Steve met with an agency art director, a young man named Rob Janoff, and gave him two projects to do for Apple Computer. One was to design a brochure that introduced the Apple II. The other was to redesign the logo. Everyone involved knew that Ron Wayne's original Darwin drawing didn't "say" what Apple was about. As Janoff recalled, the only direction he got was from Steve, who said, "Don't make it cute."

Janoff tackled the assignment in a novel way: He bought a bowlful of apples and spent a week sketching them to simplify the shape. Janoff presented two versions to Steve: a simple drawing of a whole apple and the same apple with a bite taken out of it. The latter was Janoff's favorite, because it showed the scale of the apple and offered a clear visual example of the common experience of biting into an apple. One of the biggest selling points of the Apple II was its color capability, and Janoff wanted that feature included. He simply put green on top to represent the apple's leaf. As for the rest of the rainbow colors (which are out of order), Janoff put them in the order that personally pleased him. Janoff had also learned that Steve felt strongly about introducing Apple II computers into schools, so the colors would appeal to kids as well.

Apple Computer was no longer a simple partnership agreement between Steve and Woz. On January 3, 1977, the company was formally incorporated; it was now a corporation and could offer shares of stock ownership to other investors. Apple now had a dozen employees; it moved out of the Jobses' garage and rented space in Cupertino, California.

Apple was an official, growing business, and Markkula knew that it needed a president, but he felt that neither Steve nor Woz could assume that position. Steve, soon to turn twenty-two, was too young and inexperienced. Twenty-seven-year-old Woz was too shy, an engineer at heart, and didn't want that kind of power.

Markkula turned to an acquaintance, Mike Scott,

to assume the role. Woz was delighted to welcome Scotty, as he was called, on board. Steve was less enthusiastic. For Woz, Scotty was someone who could act as a buffer to Steve, whose temperamental outbursts were occurring more frequently, and Markkula was reluctant to handle them.

One of Steve's tantrums occurred when the first batch of plastic computer cases arrived, poorly produced with uneven edges. Thankfully, there was no such problem with Rod Holt's revolutionary device. "Rod Holt designed a little circuit which took power out of the wall and let little bits of it [electrical power] in at a time," as Woz described it in an interview. Because the power wasn't constantly being fed, the computer was more efficient and didn't need a fan for cooling.

The focus now was for Apple to prepare for the West Coast Computer Faire, which was organized by some Homebrew Club members and was being held in San Francisco's Civic Auditorium that April. The Apple II would make its debut at this event.

Finally the power devices were completed, some

plastic cases were ready, computers were assembled, and the brochures and logo were ready.

But when the April date arrived, only three Apple II computers were completed. Nevertheless, Steve, Woz, Markkula, and Scotty set up the Apple booth. Markkula, guided by his philosophy of *impute*, or first impressions, paid five thousand dollars extra to get a prime spot at the convention. Unlike many of the other exhibitors, with their hand-lettered signs and card-table displays, Apple Computer looked totally professional.

Behind them hung a large illuminated Plexiglas sign with their new Apple logo displayed in brilliant color. The three Apple II computers sat on a cloth-covered table. Nearby and in plain sight were stacks of sealed Apple boxes, giving the impression that a large supply of computers was on hand. The boxes were empty.

Steve and Woz also impressed: Their hair was washed and combed, and they were clean shaven. But the biggest change? Each wore a shirt and tie to go with their three-piece suits.

8

APPLE GROWS

THE SUITS, THE DISPLAY BOOTH, and the Apple II computer all clicked. "My recollection is, we stole the show," Jobs later said. "A lot of dealers and distributors started lining up and we were off and running." The computer was advertised to go on sale April 30, 1977. That date came and went—the computers were not ready because the plastic cases had to be redone. Assembled circuit boards and other parts accumulated in Apple's offices.

Unfinished computers meant no money coming

Steve Jobs: Thinking Differently

in. But money was going out: salaries for the ever-growing staff, payments to the electrical suppliers, and fees for the outside contractors who produced the circuit boards. To ship with the Apple II, Steve also wanted to include a clearly written, well-designed manual. Mike Scott, the president, was in charge of reining in any unnecessary expenses and said no to the manual. To save money and time, Scott said they'd quickly write and type a manual and then make copies. The manual argument was only one of many between Steve and Scott.

When Scott was interviewed several years later, he recalled how Steve was stubborn and resistant to authority. Scott, just as stubborn, knew his role was to keep Steve in check. One particular fight erupted when Scott assigned employee badge numbers. Steve was given #2. Woz was given #1. Steve was furious and suggested that his badge should be #0 so that Woz could retain his number, but his own number would come first. Steve lost that argument.

But there was one he didn't lose. Apple computer buyers should be given a one-year warranty.

If anything went wrong with the computer in that first year, it would be replaced. Scott insisted that the norm—a ninety-day warranty—was sufficient. They had a rousing screaming match; Steve burst into tears. When they finally calmed down, Scott gave in. Steve's victory was a sign that he had been paying attention and wanted to implement Markkula's first principle of business—empathy for the customer.

Meanwhile, computer parts piled up, and the company's financial resources dwindled. But fortunately for Apple, it was the late seventies in Silicon Valley, and minicomputers were beginning to burst onto the scene. As a trusted businessman, Markkula was able to secure funds from investment firms to keep Apple Computer in business. These investors didn't have to wait long to see that their decisions were wise. By the end of May, the company had sold three hundred computers. And each month, the sales figures increased.

More sales meant more work, and Apple needed more employees to keep up with demand. Scott,

Markkula, and Steve were in charge of hiring. Steve often attended the interviews barefoot. With his dirty feet resting on the table, he waved away the person's résumé as unimportant, preferring to hire people by relying on his instincts.

Now that Apple was profitable and Steve was making money, he decided to move from his parents' house and rent one with Dan. When he moved in, Steve brought the only two things he felt he needed: his mattress and his meditation mat. Around this time Chrisann Brennan, Steve's high school girl-friend, returned to the area. She and Steve became a couple. But Steve didn't carve out too much time for socializing. His passion was now his work.

Of Steve's many talents, one was finding the latest technological equipment at the best price and convincing the manufacturer to adapt the device for the Apple. This ongoing search led Steve to Shugart, a company that made disk drives. Disk drives held floppy disks (which were eight inches in diameter). These disks stored more data, far more than the cassettes Woz used on the Apple I.

A disk was inserted into the drive, which was connected to the computer to upload data. But Steve wanted Shugart to make an inexpensive, five-and-a-quarter-inch floppy disk *and* the drive to go with it. With the device in hand, Woz developed the circuitry needed for it to work with the Apple II. And once Apple began selling these disk drives, sales exploded with home users and businesses who wanted a computer that had more functions.

The increasingly popular Apple II, with encouragement from the company, developed a strong fan base. As wireheads had done earlier when they formed the Homebrew Computer Club, Apple fans created informal groups where they met and discussed how they used their Apples. Fans who were software developers designed programs that they themselves wanted. If the program worked well, they could ultimately sell it to other Apple users.

Dan Bricklin was a graduate student at Harvard who would watch his professor write financial formulas in long columns on the blackboard but have to start over again if an error was made. Bricklin realized that software could be designed to do this time-consuming, tedious work. He teamed up with Bob Frankston and created the VisiCalc program, working with a small software firm. An entire spreadsheet was seen on-screen; users could enter, change, or delete data, and in seconds it would all be automatically recalculated. VisiCalc was a boon to small and large businesses. Because Bricklin and the software developers he worked with were Apple users, they designed their software solely for the Apple. Suddenly the minicomputer was no longer something for hobbyists. Because of this one particular program, small business owners could now justify the purchase of a computer—specifically, an Apple II. Woz said, "After a couple of months, the businesspeople were something like 90 percent of the market. . . . From 1,000 units a month, suddenly we went to 10,000 a month."

Steve wanted to expand Apple II's market even further. He contacted educators, who jumped at the chance to have this new technology available in their schools. Apples were now the computer of choice in middle schools, high schools, and colleges. Steve believed passionately in the power of computers as the new tool of the age—a belief also shared in his cherished *Whole Earth Catalog*. As he said in a 1985 interview, "A computer is the most incredible tool we've ever seen. It can be a writing tool, a communications center, a super calculator, a planner, a filer and an artistic instrument all in one. . . . There are no other tools that have the power and the versatility of a computer." He went on to say, "Computers have the potential to be a real breakthrough in the educational process when used in conjunction with enlightened teachers."

Mrs. Imogene "Teddy" Hill and Friar Robert Palladino would have been pleased to hear Steve extol the key ingredient in all classrooms: "enlightened teachers."

With the increasing success of Apple Computer, the company expanded and moved once again, this time to a building fifteen times larger than the last office in Cupertino. But Woz wasn't happy with the added tensions, responsibilities, and meetings that a big business brings. He became increasingly upset at Steve's many outbursts. What happened to that initial idea that Steve had fed him—start a business and have fun? Scott, too, had hoped to keep the business somewhat small. To maintain order, divisions were set up and employees reported to a division head.

Steve was frustrated with this reorganization. He also knew that the Apple II wouldn't be a hit computer forever. And the Apple II was really Woz's creation. He had to come up with some groundbreaking product that he hoped would change the world. He proceeded to push for the Apple III—a computer intended to enter the business arena and prove that Apple could do more than balance checkbooks and play games. But with a price tag of four thousand dollars, and no internal cooling fan—among other problems—the Apple III flopped. According to Woz, "the Apple III was not developed by a single engineer. . . . It was developed by committee, by the marketing department."

But Steve was already onto another idea. He wanted to create a computer far more powerful than the Apple II. He called this computer Lisa. Lisa was the name of Steve and Chrisann's daughter. Now that the couple was no longer together, Steve didn't see Lisa, but perhaps naming the computer for her was his attempt to show he cared. Trip Hawkins, one of the Lisa team members, recalls Steve saying about the Lisa, "Let's make a dent in the universe. We'll make it so important that it will make a dent in the universe."

At the same time Steve was developing Lisa, another team of Apple engineers was working on a new computer, the Macintosh. They felt they were developing groundbreaking technology and didn't want their project to get shelved. There was one big problem: Jef Raskin, the man in charge, was not one of Steve's favorites. In fact, Steve considered him a "bozo" and dismissed his work. Jef was one of many Steve couldn't tolerate. More and more, without giving people a chance, Steve made quick judgments and labeled people either "brilliant" or "bozos."

Jef wasn't willing to give up his work on the Macintosh. He and the others on the team came up with a plan. Some Macintosh team members convinced Steve to visit the Xerox company's Palo Alto Research Center (known as Xerox PARC) in December 1979. Xerox kept their developments under wraps, but engineers at Apple had a good idea of what was going on. Most importantly, Macintosh engineers sensed that the work Xerox was doing was similar to what they themselves were developing.

Steve and the few people he took with him were shown everything being developed for the computer at Xerox PARC. Steve got the chance to look for himself: Xerox had approached him about investing in Apple. He told them they could invest $1 million if they let him tour PARC and shared their secrets. Steve couldn't contain himself, he was so excited by what he saw. When he and his crew drove away, he told his car mates he believed what they'd just witnessed was the future of computers. Steve also couldn't believe what he'd observed—that the people at Xerox's headquarters back east didn't have a clue as to how exciting and revolutionary Xerox PARC's work was.

What was it that made Steve so excited? He'd seen a computer with graphics on its screen, called

PATRICIA LAKIN

graphical user interface (GUI, or "gooey"). Instead of typing words to direct the computer to a specific file, the user could point to a picture of the file on the screen. Point? That was the other new development Steve saw that day—a hand-controlled pointer, called a mouse. It was simple, instinctive, fantastic.

Steve went back to Apple and immediately wanted to create what he'd just seen . . . only simpler and better.

As for Xerox's mouse, it had three buttons on the top, each with a different function. Steve wanted Apple's mouse to be far smaller and simpler. He hired a designer and gave the order to make a mouse with only two control buttons and a ball underneath so it could roll on a table or a pant leg. Steve's crew knew they had to deliver.

The Macintosh team must have given a sigh of relief. Their project wouldn't be eliminated now that Steve shared their vision. GUI technology was the new frontier for computers.

While Steve and the Macintosh team went to work, businessmen far from California were hard at work for Apple. There were plans to take the company public (that is, to sell pieces of ownership in the company), and that meant anyone who had money and wanted to could buy a share in Apple stock.

The day of the initial public offering, or IPO, was scheduled for December 12, 1980. A price was established at twenty-two dollars per share. If many people bought the stock, it also meant the price could go up. The people who already owned shares in the company—like the largest stockholders, Steve, Woz, Scott, Markkula, and others—could become very rich in a matter of hours.

So many people bought Apple's stock that the price shot up to twenty-nine dollars per share. On that December day, twenty-five-year-old Steve Jobs—third-grade terror, Reed College dropout, meditator, fruit eater, Bob Dylan fan, a young man whose company had started in his parents' garage— was now worth $265 million.

PATRICIA LAKIN

9

APPLE'S STAR

THE APPLE COMPUTER IPO WAS THE largest in US corporate history since 1956, when the Ford Motor Company first listed its shares. More than forty Apple employees became millionaires that day. But Dan Kottke—Steve's old friend, former roommate, and one of the first Apple employees—wasn't one of them. He'd been asking Steve for months about getting stock in the company before it went public. Steve kept brushing Dan off.

Another longtime employee, Rod Holt, learned

that Dan hadn't been included in the stock options. So he approached Steve and suggested they each give him an equal number of shares from their own vast amount. Steve replied that he'd give Dan "zero" shares.

Woz was distressed about the employees who didn't receive shares. He personally sold some of his stocks to Dan and others at a fair price so they could reap the rewards of their loyalty and hard work.

While Dan bore no grudge, he was puzzled by Steve's behavior. If Steve had acted out of anger, he never shared that fact with Dan. To this day, Steve's action remains a mystery to him.

By the age of twenty-five, Steve had superstar status after becoming a multimillionaire. He was on the cover of *Inc.* and later *Time* magazine.

He bought his own house in Los Gatos, and even though he could certainly afford to furnish it, he didn't. Choosing furniture meant selecting items that fit his sense of style and design. Not much did. His living room was "furnished" with sound equipment, a bookcase half-filled with books, an original Tiffany lamp, and his meditation mat. His bedroom was equally as sparse—it contained his mattress and, on the walls, black-and-white photos of the guru he had hoped to meet, Neem Karoli Baba, and the famous physicist Albert Einstein.

The massive success did nothing to calm Steve. At work he was more temperamental than ever. He was put on the Lisa Computer team but then removed. Next, it was the Macintosh team. He was excited by their work and wanted to lead their group. However, Jef Raskin already headed the team, and he and Steve had intense disagreements about the direction of the Macintosh.

Jef wanted to make this computer truly affordable, which meant selecting certain inexpensive parts over others to keep down the cost. And even though Jef wanted to incorporate graphics in the computer, he didn't feel that all the innovative features they'd seen at PARC were essential. He was ready to use a less expensive microprocessor, eliminate many of the graphics, and do away with the mouse. Steve was appalled. He felt that using graphics for application windows with pull-down menus, controlled by using the mouse, was absolutely critical. Jef differed and wasn't impressed by Steve's star power. Their conflicts became personal as well as professional, and increasingly more disruptive. Steve wanted to assemble his own crew and take over the Macintosh project.

Mike Scott, the president, reluctantly stepped in. He summoned Steve and Jef into his office with Markkula present. As he had done before, Steve burst into tears. Scott had already ousted Steve from the Lisa project. This time he let Steve win. He'd take over and Jef was invited to take a leave of absence. Jef agreed—and took a permanent one from Apple.

Some may have felt that Steve's outbursts were due to his sense of style and design and expectations of how things should be done. But others at Apple were equally passionate. They could get along with their coworkers. For no apparent reason, Steve would reject or turn on people. He wasn't an easy puzzle for those around him to decipher.

Steve assembled his Macintosh team and insisted they move to a different site, away from the main office building. They named their new space Texaco

PATRICIA LAKIN

Towers, because their building was close to a Texaco gas station. As Steve recalled, "It was like going back to the garage for me. I had my own ragtag team and I was in control."

Steve hoped Woz could join the team, but Woz had been spending less and less time at Apple. He'd used the money he made from the IPO to buy a plane and take flying lessons. Sadly, in February 1981, his plane crashed shortly after takeoff. Woz barely survived and needed a very long recuperation time.

Steve invited Apple employees working on other projects to join him, but he asked only those he felt were brilliant. "Bozos" were left out. When someone new was interviewed, Steve would slowly pull off the cover of the prototype Macintosh and watch for the interviewee's reaction. If the person just looked, they weren't a candidate. On the other hand, if the person began using the mouse and interacting with what they were seeing on the computer screen, that person was immediately hired.

At work in Texaco Towers, Steve shouted, cursed, cajoled, and pushed his team to work harder, longer,

Steve Jobs: Thinking Differently

and better. But an intriguing development occurred with that crew—they learned how to deal with Steve. They even had an annual award (which they suspected Steve knew of) for the team member who'd done the best job of standing up to Steve the most in a given year. One of the team members realized that when Steve stared at someone's final product and declared it garbage, his insult was a coded message: What he really wanted was proof that this was the best approach. Oftentimes the criticized team member understood that if he or she tried a little harder, an even better device or plan of attack could be produced. There was one other element that made this crew work together so seamlessly: They shared Steve's passion and drive to produce a truly awesome, groundbreaking computer.

That didn't mean they all agreed with one another. One particular day Steve faced off with a team member who wanted to create the windows (the areas on the screen that display their own files or messages) for these computers as "absolute rectangles." Steve wanted rectangles with curved edges. The discussion of rectangles with or without rounded edges went on for quite a while.

His desire for curved edges went back to his childhood and his father's love for the classic lines of some of his favorite model cars—many sported curved edges. Steve told the team that rounded edges were everywhere. He pointed to tables, chairs, and other objects around the room. To finally settle the dispute, he took the employee for a walk outside. He pointed out car lines, all curved. When Steve pointed to the rounded corners on the No Parking sign, the team member gave up and conceded the argument. This was a revolutionary design concept.

Steve also insisted that the Macintosh have different styles of fonts—or styles of lettering. He'd not forgotten his class at Reed with Friar Palladino. One designer who was hired to work on those fonts came up with the trash can icon to signify, naturally, "trash."

Even the circuit board had to be beautiful. Steve required the chips to be perfectly aligned, and the wiring had to be done in straight lines. When one technician objected and said no one would know, Steve told him that *he* would know. He recalled his dad's lesson that a cabinetmaker makes a beautiful wooden cabinet on all sides, even the one that sits against the wall that no one can see.

Steve worked his crew endlessly to have them design the most stylish computer casing possible. Many opposed his insistence on making very minor changes that they weren't able to notice. To prove them wrong, Steve displayed all their prototype versions so they could see how small changes could make a big difference.

Outside Texaco Towers, Apple's president, Mike Scott, was encountering difficulties. In February 1981, due to the Apple III failure, Mike Scott had to personally lay off forty employees in what became known as Black Wednesday. Several months later he resigned.

Although Markkula temporarily assumed Scott's duties as president and Jobs became chairman, it was two years until a permanent replacement was found. Steve became acquainted with John Sculley, the man who headed PepsiCo. Both Sculley and Steve held high-level positions in their respective companies, but their personalities were totally different. Sculley was quiet and polite. Despite this, they grew to like each other as friends, and Steve felt Sculley was the perfect choice to be the new president. However, Sculley wasn't interested in leaving PepsiCo. When Steve asked him whether he wanted to sell soda forever or work for a company that was part of the future, Sculley was finally swayed, and he became Apple's new president in 1983. "If you can pick one reason why I came to Apple, it was to have the chance to work with Steve," Sculley said at the time.

Also in 1983, the race was on (at least in Steve's mind) between the Macintosh and the Lisa. He hoped the Macintosh would debut first, but it wasn't ready. The Lisa was. As the most famous face of Apple, Steve was in charge of the Lisa's press conference. Sculley asked that Steve not mention the Macintosh (Steve's own pet project). Steve couldn't help himself. He introduced the Lisa but basically indicated that the soon-to-be-released Macintosh would *really* be spectacular. Sculley was far from amused.

The Lisa was designed as a high-end computer and had a hefty price tag of $16,000. Because of its price and the idea that a better computer would come along, sales of the Lisa fell far short of the company's projections.

All the Macintosh changes that Steve demanded took time and extra expense. The team dreamed of giving it a price tag of just under a thousand dollars. Steve did the calculations and realized that it would have to sell for $1,995 to be profitable. But Sculley didn't accept Steve's figures and insisted that another five hundred dollars be added to the retail price. The Mac team was furious because, at that price, it was a betrayal to their customers. Furthermore, Sculley was not impressed with Steve's product or design and was concerned with how the company could make a profit. Steve lost that battle. Their friendship became strained; Steve realized that he and Sculley didn't have the same vision for Apple.

The Macintosh was finally ready at the start of

1984. Steve wanted it to have a spectacular release. Regis McKenna, Apple's advertising agency, had recently joined the much larger Chiat/Day. The ad agency, like Steve, wanted a television commercial that would be truly bold and original and make a statement. Apple bought television time to air the ad during halftime of the 1984 Super Bowl (Los Angeles Raiders vs. Washington Redskins). Ridley Scott, the director of the hit movie *Blade Runner*, was selected to film the commercial for a budget of $900,000. The ad agency decided to use a theme from a book written thirty-five years before, George Orwell's futuristic novel *1984*. Blank-faced people are focused on a giant screen, projecting a Big Brother figure. A woman wielding a hammer hurls it and smashes the screen. Then a voice-over is heard: "On January 24, Apple Computer will introduce Macintosh. And you'll see why 1984 won't be like *1984*." The message was clear: The Macintosh computer would break the robotic mold of all other computers. It *would* put a dent in the universe.

Sculley saw the commercial before it aired and

was horrified. He demanded the television time be sold off and the commercial never shown. Steve and his team were totally wowed. As it turned out, the commercial was aired, and everyone from newscasters to sportswriters to the viewing public was blown away. (The commercial went on to win many prestigious awards, including Best Super Bowl Spot, bestowed in 2007 to commemorate the Super Bowl's fortieth anniversary.)

Days later, in the packed Flint Auditorium in Cupertino, at the annual shareholders meeting, Steve revealed the Macintosh. His crew sat in the front rows wearing Macintosh T-shirts. The lights dimmed and Steve—in bowtie and jacket—appeared in a spotlight. He brought out a case and set it on a table. Welcoming the audience, he quoted Bob Dylan, "The times they are a changin'," and the show began. Slowly he lifted the Macintosh out of its case, turned it on, and one by one, in majestic letters, M A C I N T O S H whisked across the computer screen. On a starlit background, under the word MACINTOSH, the words INSANELY GREAT! were magically inscribed. The crowd roared.

In succession, MacWrite, the fonts, MacDraw, and a game of chess appeared. The crowd went wild and gave this computer and Steve a standing ovation.

But the show wasn't over. Now it was time for the Macintosh to *speak* for itself. "Hello, I am Macintosh. It sure is great to get out of that bag." And then the Macintosh concluded, "So it is with considerable pride that I introduce a man who's been like a father to me, Steve Jobs." Once again, the crowd roared. But Steve focused on the people in the first five rows. Like him, they were overcome with emotion. All their efforts had truly paid off. They cheered as they wept for joy.

After the Macintosh's spectacular debut, Steve became even more of a celebrity. In 1985 he turned thirty, and in keeping with his star power, he threw himself a lavish party at a large San Francisco hotel. The legendary singer Ella Fitzgerald was hired to entertain. This type of showiness was a far cry from the young man who walked around Reed's campus barefoot and walked seven miles to get free food from Portland's Hare Krishna temple.

After the initial "Mac-mania" died down, reality

set in. Sales began to flatten out. The Apple work-force was bickering and divided over favored treat-ment and salaries and Steve.

Steve felt bound in and restricted by John Sculley and disliked his emphasis on creating profits rather than beautiful products. Steve decided that he'd force the issue with the company's board of directors, tell-ing them he couldn't continue to work with Sculley. They had to choose between them. The board was becoming increasingly bothered by Steve's abrasive-ness and wanted Sculley to stand up to Steve. They made their choice. It *wasn't* Steve.

Steve Jobs, cofounder of Apple Computer, was not fired. But he was told that he wasn't going to be on any team. He was given an office but with no depart-ment to head and nothing to do. "I'd get there, and I would have one or two phone calls to perform, a little bit of mail to look at. . . . A few people might see my car in the parking lot and come over and commiser-ate. And I would get depressed and go home in two or three or four hours, really depressed."

Steve had heard of two start-up companies: One

PATRICIA LAKIN

Steve Jobs: Thinking Differently

did work with flat-screen technology, and the other was working on touch-screen displays. These new concepts fortified Steve, and he suggested that he'd create a lab to work on new products. Sculley and the board were firm: no. Steve burst into tears.

On September 17, 1985, Steve wrote his letter of resignation. Nine years before, he'd signed a piece of paper that started this company. Now he composed a letter that ended his ties to Apple Computer. Both times, he signed his name in exactly the same way: *steven p. jobs.*

10

WHAT'S NEXT?

T WAS A DEVASTATING TURN OF EVENTS FOR Steve not to be part of Apple. Without his company and his team, he was an artist with no canvas and no paints. He definitely saw himself as an artist, one who created innovative products.

One year earlier Steve had told his Macintosh team that great artists sign their work. When the Macintosh was finally finished, he'd asked them all to sign their names on a piece of paper. The signatures, including Steve's, were then copied and permanently engraved on the inside casing of each Macintosh computer.

Customers wouldn't know the signatures were there, but each artist who created the Macintosh would.

In 1985 Steve was cut out from Apple—cut off from his team and the company he'd founded and grown into a major corporation. He described how he felt: "You've probably had somebody punch you in the stomach and it knocks the wind out of you and you can't breathe. If you relax you'll start breathing again. That's how I felt. . . . The thing I had to do was try to relax. It was hard. But I went for a lot of long walks in the woods and didn't really talk to a lot of people."

"Do you know what you want to do with the rest of this lifetime?" an interviewer asked Steve that same year. His answer was, "There's an old Hindu saying that comes into my mind occasionally: For the first thirty years of your life, you make your habits. For the last thirty years of your life, your habits make you. . . . If you want to live your life in a creative way, as an artist, you have to not look back too much."

In 1985 the world was filled with second acts and renewals, some resounding successes, others with mixed results: President Reagan was sworn in for a second term, having won forty-nine of fifty states. Tina Turner, a legendary rock-and-roll singer, had the comeback of the year, winning a Grammy for "What's Love Got to Do With It." The Coca-Cola company shelved their classic formula and came out with New Coke, a fabulous failure. Gamers everywhere rejoiced when Nintendo Entertainment System introduced Super Mario Bros. into homes.

Steve was thirty years old. And to his way of thinking that meant looking ahead and finding the chance to create even more truly great products—but what? What would his next act be?

He had always been a champion of computers in the classroom. Starting in the late seventies, Apple formed the Apple Education Foundation, followed by The Kids Can't Wait and then the Apple University Consortium. The programs either donated computers to schools or provided computer support and offered discounts to the schools and colleges that purchased Apples.

In conjunction with these projects, Steve visited Stanford University and met Paul Berg, a Nobel

Prize–winning biochemist. Steve had become interested in gene research and Berg's work in that area. Berg explained that his research work was exciting but evaluating the data was a long, time-consuming process. What about using computer programs to help calculate all that data? Steve asked. Berg confirmed that there was no computer for that kind of scientific evaluation.

That was it—Steve had his new course: He'd start a computer company specifically designed for scientists and people in higher education. He'd develop the hardware—the actual computer—and work to find or create the required software. He'd link the computers to one another for ease in sharing files and data. For the first time in a while, Steve was energized. He spoke to some of his former Apple team members, several of whom wanted to join this innovative new venture. The news that Apple would be losing several key employees energized John Sculley as well—with outrage.

Steve responded in a *Newsweek* interview: "There is nothing, by the way, that says Apple can't compete with us if they think what we're doing is such a great idea. It is hard to think that a $2 billion company [Apple] with 4,300-plus people couldn't compete with six people in blue jeans."

Steve sold all his Apple shares save one. That one share allowed him to continue to be a stockholder and attend the annual stockholders' meetings. With the sale of almost 6.5 million shares, Steve now had $100 million to use for his new start-up. He decided to call his new company NeXT.

When conceptualizing NeXT, Steve remembered, believed in, and applied Markkula's mantra, *You do judge a book by its cover.* He wanted the company to have a distinctive presence. Steve hired renowned graphic designer Paul Rand (for a fee of $100,000) to design the company logo. Jobs wanted this computer to be cube-shaped, so Rand encased NeXT's four letters in a tilted, two-dimensional cube with only the *e* in lowercase. The company's headquarters in Redwood City, California, were renovated with polished wood floors, large glass windows, and at the building's entrance, a staircase designed by noted architect I. M. Pei that appeared as if it were floating. There were no closed offices—everyone worked at desks in a large, open common space.

As Steve assembled his team, he kept many of the same off-hour traditions he'd instituted with the Macintosh team: late-night company pizza parties, and weekend retreats to get away from work and relax. But the rest of the time, the on-site working conditions were also the same: ninety-hour work-weeks, accompanied by Steve's sudden angry outbursts as well as his sporadic praise.

As Steve had said, habits are formed by age thirty. His style at work hadn't changed. At meetings, with everyone seated around a table, Steve could be found in his chair—but not actually sitting. He'd be kneeling or slouched down like a little kid. If he wasn't at the table, he'd be up and about, forever moving around the room. He'd be biting his nails or scribbling on a blackboard. His eyes could bore into someone who was speaking, making them feel uncomfortable. Or he'd roll his eyes at the speaker to show his utter frustration with them.

Steve's perfectionism and habit of obsessing over minor details didn't change either. The cube that he'd insisted on for the case was costly to produce. The size also meant the circuit boards couldn't be constructed on one flat board, but needed to be stacked one on top of the other in order to fit. These design refinements were costly and caused delays. Delays meant there were no NeXT computers to sell. With nothing to sell, there was no revenue for the company.

After a few years of NeXT earning nothing, and Steve's reputation as a brilliant businessman in question, he needed funding to keep the company afloat. Keeping the company alive meant keeping his reputation alive as well. Luckily for Steve, an appearance on television saved him: A PBS documentary, *Entrepreneurs*, included a piece on Steve and his new company. A billionaire Texas businessman, Ross Perot, watched the show and liked what he saw. Perot came to the rescue. His excellent reputation in the business world and his $20 million investment put NeXT and Steve on stronger footing. Perot said, "Steve and his whole

NeXT team are the darndest bunch of perfectionists I've ever seen."

Steve also needed software applications, so he approached an old acquaintance, Bill Gates. Years earlier, Bill's software company, Microsoft, had worked with the Macintosh team and their GUI-based software to develop applications for the Macintosh. Later Gates came up with a version of that GUI application software that he incorporated into his own product, Windows. Now wildly successful himself, Bill didn't need the work. Moreover, he didn't think much of Steve's new computer and didn't mind sharing his opinion publicly. Steve was furious at the bad press and thought Gates was completely wrong. Steve knew his software program, NeXTSTEP, was revolutionary, and software vendors would be clamoring for the chance to develop applications for it. At that moment, none were knocking on his door.

NeXT's computer was way behind schedule. But Steve knew the power of presentation, so he arranged for a spectacular launch of NeXT and its software (even though the computer *still* wasn't finished), at

Symphony Hall in San Francisco, on October 12, 1988. "We've built the best computer in the world," Jobs had said a few days earlier. "Every computer will be different from now on." Perot agreed: "They spent an inordinate amount of time striving for perfection. He's done it again."

This computer would be the first to contain an entire dictionary and the complete works of William Shakespeare. Essentially, Steve had created the first truly digital book. At the presentation's conclusion, the assembled audience of three thousand college and university administrators and educators, software developers, and reporters heard the price: $6,500. They gasped. The printer would be an additional $2,000. The potential buyers had hoped the entire package would sell for $2,500.

When NeXT computers finally rolled off the assembly line, Steve hoped they'd sell ten thousand a month. Instead only about four hundred were sold each month.

One reporter asked Steve why the computer was so late. Steve responded, "It's not late. It's five years ahead of its time." Once again, Steve was right. In 1989 a noted computer scientist, Tim Berners-Lee, worked on a NeXT computer and its NeXTSTEP software to develop a web server and web browser. Two years later it went online, and the world now knew of Berners-Lee's work and the birth of the Internet.

The NeXT computer was only one of Steve's new passions after he left Apple. His second love was working at Pixar, the computer animation film studio. George Lucas, creator of *Star Wars*, was Pixar's original owner. In 1986 Steve bought the company for $10 million. What attracted Steve to Pixar? First, their software was totally integrated, meaning it was compatible only with their Pixar Image Computers. Steve strongly believed in total integration between hardware and software, and that was exactly how he'd designed NeXT computers. Second, their software amazed him. Its images could be rendered in 3-D, which made it an ideal tool for animators, graphic designers, and even for the medical community in performing scans. And third, heading Pixar's animation department was John Lasseter, an artist.

For Steve, working with this crew was a perfect marriage of technology and art.

Despite the $125,000 price tag of the Pixar Image Computer, Steve thought a lower-priced version of this machine (with its software) could be sold to the public. He soon realized it was *way* beyond the average person's reach. But it wasn't beyond the reach of a major animation movie studio, Disney. They purchased the computers and software to create the last scene in their 1988 blockbuster movie, *The Little Mermaid.*

Even with Disney as a customer, along with other animation and graphic design studios, sales at Pixar were poor. Steve had to invest more and more of his own money to keep Pixar solvent. His reputation as a clever, insightful businessman was taking a beating from his involvement with Pixar and NeXT. But he wasn't ready to give up on either one.

During one meeting at Pixar, Steve suggested to Lasseter that he make a short animated film to enter into a competition that would showcase the computer's capabilities. Lasseter's desk was covered

PATRICIA LAKIN

with small toys and a Luxo lamp. He used the image of his lamp for the film and created a story about two lamps playing with a ball. When Lasseter's film, *Luxo Jr.*, was shown at SIGGRAPH, the computer graphics industry's largest convention, it got a standing ovation and won an award as best film. Edwin Catmull, Pixar's chief technical officer, said of the film, "*Luxo Jr.* sent shock waves through the entire industry—to all corners of computer and traditional animation. At that time, most traditional artists were afraid of the computer. They did not realize that the computer was merely a different tool in the artist's kit but instead perceived it as a type of automation that might endanger their jobs. Luckily, this attitude changed dramatically in the early '80s with the use of personal computers in the home."

The film's success brought a few jobs for animated commercials, but it didn't lead to sales of Pixar's computer with its magical software. Steve had to cut staff and expenses to stay afloat. At one cost-cutting meeting, even Lasseter was hesitant to ask Steve if he could have $300,000 to complete another of his films. Despite the cuts, Steve agreed to finance the short film but warned Lasseter that it better be good. Lasseter created a short animated film entitled *Tin Toy*. It featured a looming baby that scares its newest toy, a tin one-man band. That year, 1988, *Tin Toy* won an Academy Award for best animated short. Lasseter thanked his crew and Steve Jobs and noted that it was the first-ever computer-animated film to win an Academy Award.

Steve's trust in Lasseter proved correct. Following this success, Disney approached Lasseter, asking him to work for them and direct an animated film about toys. With his short film, Disney recognized the powerful attraction of animated toys for children's entertainment. Lasseter thought at Disney he'd only be a director. If he stayed at Pixar with Steve, he'd make history. His loyalty to Steve and his passion for his art were too great for him to ever consider leaving Pixar.

Since Lasseter wouldn't come to Disney, they approached Steve *and* Lasseter and asked if Pixar would make a movie about toys for them. They said yes. The compelling story starred Woody, a toy cowboy, and Buzz Lightyear, an astronaut action figure. While Lasseter worked on the script, he had many meetings with Disney, who wanted the story to be more edgy with more conflict.

Woody was made a bit mean, spiteful, and very jealous of Buzz. In 1993 Lasseter brought the first half of the film to Disney. After the screening, they picked it apart, and Lasseter himself was upset by what he'd created. Tom Hanks, who'd been signed for the voice of Woody, thought that Woody was a real jerk.

Lasseter scratched everything he had and went back to the beginning. He rewrote the story the way he'd wanted to tell it: Kindhearted Woody, Andy's favorite toy, feels displaced when Buzz, a new action figure toy, comes along. Released in November 1995, Pixar's *Toy Story* was the first full-length movie ever to be made with computer-generated imagery (CGI). It went on to sell $191 million in tickets in the United States and Canada and $361 million in ticket sales worldwide. It has since spun off movie sequels and numerous toys.

When Steve started NeXT in 1986, he nurtured that company along for years. But it was proving to be a failure—until he changed course and focused on selling software programs that eventually turned NeXT's fortunes around. After almost ten years of no success with Pixar, Steve finally had a hit. His belief in the success of this computer-animated technology was publicly acknowledged.

One week after *Toy Story*'s release, Steve took Pixar's stock public. The initial price was set at $22 a share. By the end of the selling day, the stock settled at $39 per share. Steve's stock was worth $1.2 billion. But as he said then, "I've never done this for the money." Steve had one motivation: He worked passionately to create a product that he truly believed would have an enduring impact. According to business writer David A. Price, "Steve's major impact was on the strategic direction of the company. He had the crucial insight that Pixar could one day be the equal of the Walt Disney Company in animation."

Pixar and Lasseter were the perfect match for Steve. That relationship gave him the opportunity to integrate art and technology *and* revolutionize the movie industry.

11

MEANWHILE . . .

NeXT AND PIXAR PROVIDED STEVE with a sense of family and occupied a great deal of his time. Nevertheless, he was curious to learn about his biological parents. Unbeknownst to Paul and Clara, he had years earlier contacted a private detective—but no details turned up.

In the mid-1980s, Clara was diagnosed with lung cancer. She had been a smoker. Steve spent a great deal of time with his mother at her deathbed, and it was only then that he asked for details about his adoption. There is no indication Clara was able to provide any clues. So he carefully studied his birth certificate. The doctor who had delivered him had signed it, and apparently had arranged for his adoption. Once again, Steve trusted the area telephone directory and found the doctor's name and number. He called and asked for information.

The doctor apologized to Steve, saying he couldn't help because all his records had been lost in a fire. Shortly afterward, Steve found out the doctor hadn't been truthful. After Steve's call, the doctor wrote a letter to him; on the outside of the envelope were instructions to deliver the letter to Steve Jobs upon the doctor's death. He died shortly after Steve contacted him, but the information Steve had been searching for was in that letter: the names of his biological parents.

He chose not to hire another detective to find them until after his mother died. He loved Clara and Paul deeply and didn't want either one to feel slighted by his search in any way. Clara Jobs died in 1986. At that point, Steve approached his dad and asked for permission to seek out his biological parents. Paul encouraged him to do so.

Steve subsequently located and contacted his biological mother, whose name was now Joanne Simpson. They met in Los Angeles, Joanne's current home. He was surprised to learn from her that he had a sister, Mona. She was two years younger than he was and lived in New York City, where she was at work on her first novel. Steve was ecstatic that she was an artist. He also discovered that his biological father had left Joanne and Mona shortly after Mona's birth, and they later divorced. After that, Joanne married George Simpson, and Mona took his last name. However, Joanne and George also eventually divorced. In contrast to Steve's stable and loving family life with Paul and Clara and his sister Patty, Joanne and Mona's lives sounded difficult. What would his life have been like had he not been adopted?

Joanne told Steve she'd been heartbroken to give him up. But he assured her that his parents and the home they'd made for him were terrific. After their meeting, Joanne and Steve flew to New York to meet Mona.

Mona recalled meeting Steve in the lobby of a New York City hotel. After the three of them talked, Steve asked Mona if they could be alone. He then took her on a long walk. It was exactly the kind of activity Mona enjoyed. They discovered how similar they were: both had intense personalities, were attentive to the tiniest details of their surroundings, and were passionate about their work. It was the beginning of a close relationship between the two siblings.

The day-to-day complications and struggles of NeXT and Pixar consumed Steve, but he tried to carve out more time to spend with his daughter, Lisa. And to date. However, there was no one he felt was special enough, or who could understand him, or put up with his intense mood swings—attentive one moment, absorbed only with work the next.

One October day in 1989, Steve was scheduled to give a lecture to graduate students at Stanford

PATRICIA LAKIN

University's Graduate School of Business. While waiting to be introduced, he took a seat at the front of the auditorium. Soon after, Laurene Powell, a tall, young, blond woman, sat beside him. She struck up a conversation, not realizing he was the speaker she'd come to hear. Steve was captivated, and fortunately, Laurene was taken with him as well.

When his lecture was over, Steve approached her and asked if they could have dinner on Saturday. She agreed. Steve headed to his car to drive to a scheduled meeting but suddenly thought, why should he wait until Saturday? Why not ask her to dinner now? He raced from his car and found Laurene, who told him that she'd be delighted to join him for an organic vegetarian dinner—Steve's food of choice.

Workaholic Steve's snap decision to ditch the meeting and have dinner with Laurene went along with a philosophy he'd held since he was a teenager: "Since [the age of seventeen], I have looked in the mirror every morning and asked myself: 'If today were the last day of my life, would I want to do what I am about to do today?' And whenever the answer

Steve Jobs: Thinking Differently

has been 'no' for too many days in a row, I know I need to change something." After meeting Laurene, he asked himself that same question and answered that he'd rather be with her than at the meeting.

Laurene Powell and Steven P. Jobs were married on March 18, 1991, at the Ahwahnee Hotel in Yosemite National Park. Steve's dad, Paul, stood proudly by his son's side. Family and friends gathered (even Steve's newly discovered sister, Mona) as Steve's Zen teacher, Kobun Chino Otogawa, performed the marriage ceremony, using a gong and incense.

Steve and Laurene bought a one-story brick house in Palo Alto, on a tree-lined street surrounded by other unpretentious houses. While Steve's other, larger home still had few furnishings, Laurene insisted on having a bed, some dressers, and a few chairs.

Work, of course, never stopped for Steve, but he and Laurene created a solid home life for themselves, which provided a needed buffer and balance to Steve's hectic schedule. Their first child, born in 1991, was a boy, whom they named Reed Paul; their daughter Erin was born three years later; and Eve, four years after that. When she was fourteen, Lisa moved in with Steve, Laurene, and their family, as she was having a difficult time with her mom, Chrisann. Lisa lived with them until she left to attend Harvard University.

Steve was a multimillionaire, able to afford whatever money could buy. However, for the twenty years they were married, the Jobs family had no servants, chauffeur, or security guards, and often, not even locked doors. Anyone walking down the street could peer into Steve's house. His belief in simplicity in design also extended to his lifestyle.

The 1990s were pivotal years for the global expansion of computer use in both the home and business. The Internet allowed the network of computers to connect all over the world and let people communicate with one another in a completely different and exciting way. It was a new "online" world—with e-mail, games, and software—and it was growing by leaps and bounds.

While Steve was busy helping raise his family,

working at NeXT, and staying on top of the business end at Pixar, he also kept up with the news of Apple Computer. During the nineties, Apple's fortunes shifted. The Apple II was no longer the hot seller it had once been, which was exactly what Steve had predicted and why he'd worked so hard to develop the next generation of computers: the Lisa and the Macintosh. The Macintosh (and the laser printer that came out a bit later) revolutionized desktop publishing: its fonts, easy-to-use software, and superior graphics made it the computer of choice for graphic artists, designers, and publishing professionals. But sales were slow. Apple Computer was no longer an innovator—it had stagnated.

Bill Gates's company, Microsoft, was fantastically successful in selling their GUI-based operating system, Windows, to all the other computer companies. Apple continued to lose ground because computer users (and software developers) were turning to machines with Microsoft's operating system already installed. To make matters worse, Apple computers were generally more expensive. In 1995 Microsoft

Steve Jobs: Thinking Differently

launched Windows 95, their best product to date. People reasoned, why should they buy an Apple computer, which cost more and ran fewer applications? IBM's computers and Windows operating system completely dominated the market.

Steve owned only one share of stock, so Apple's plunging price didn't affect his finances. What hurt him deeply was the company's loss of standing, as it was no longer in the forefront as a pioneer. In a 1985 interview, Steve said, "To me, Apple exists in the spirit of the people who work there, and the sort of philosophies and purpose by which they go about their business. So if Apple just becomes a place where computers are a commodity item and where the romance is gone, and where people forget that computers are the most incredible invention that man has ever invented, then I'll feel I have lost Apple. But if I'm a million miles away and all those people still feel those things and they're still working to make the next great personal computer, then I will feel that my genes are still in there."

John Sculley was long gone as Apple's president.

In an attempt to turn the company around, Apple's board of directors kept hiring and then firing presidents. Gil Amelio, their latest hire, started at Apple in February 1996. He faced considerable problems the moment he stepped in as CEO. Sales and the stock price were both plummeting. Talented people were leaving the company. In addition, Apple's promised new operating system was behind schedule, complex, and unreliable.

Amelio needed a better operating system—the software that is the computer's master control panel—for Apple and needed it fast. Steve was unaware that some of his top software developers at NeXT had contacted Apple. They were convinced their product (NeXTSTEP) was exactly what Apple needed. When Steve learned what they'd done, he was surprised at their initiative and pleased with their pride.

In early December 1996, Steve made his presentation of NeXTSTEP to Amelio and other Apple executives. Steve was still a master showman and salesperson. A *New York Times* journalist wrote, "On a desktop computer, he showed four video clips simultaneously, including Apple advertisements. His message: NeXT's orphaned operating system was still five to seven years ahead of its time. It would especially appeal to Internet and applications programmers."

On December 20, Apple and NeXT reached an agreement: Apple would buy NeXT for $377.5 million, plus 1.5 million Apple shares, which went to Steve. Along with the company came Steve, as an informal adviser. In a statement released the night Apple purchased NeXT, Jobs wrote, "Much of the industry has lived off the Macintosh for over ten years now, slowly copying the Mac's revolutionary user interface. Now the time has come for new innovation, and where better than Apple for this to spring from? . . . With this merger, the advanced software from NeXT will be married with Apple's very high-volume hardware platforms and marketing channels to create another breakthrough, leapfrogging existing platforms, and fueling Apple and the industry copycats for the next ten years and beyond. I still have very deep feelings for Apple, and it gives me great joy to play a role in architecting Apple's future."

In Steve's advisory capacity, he saw firsthand how desperate a situation Apple was in. Key people kept quitting; the company was hemorrhaging money, having lost close to $1.6 billion.

By June 1997 the Apple board was given the stark financial figures. Apple had suffered one of the biggest quarterly losses in Silicon Valley history. The board realized that they had a 60 percent chance of saving the company if they did two things: fire Amelio and ask Steve to come back.

Early one Monday morning, Amelio addressed the top Apple executives to announce that he was no longer CEO. Fred Anderson, acting CEO, told the assembled crowd that Steve would be directing business from behind the scenes. Steve came onstage, wearing shorts, sneakers, and a black turtleneck. He said to the crowd, "Okay, tell me what's wrong with this place." Without waiting for a response, he went on to say that the products stunk.

This forcefulness and directness didn't sound like the tone of a part-time adviser. They sounded like the man who'd put his heart and soul into this company. It was clear: He wasn't taking any backseat role to bring his "child" back to health.

First, Steve told the executive team that the current board of directors had to be asked to resign. In his opinion, most of them, along with Amelio and past presidents, had had a hand in driving Apple into the ground. He made it clear that if he could not get the majority of the board members to resign, he would leave immediately. The executives felt that Steve Jobs was the one who could turn everything around.

Steve didn't want to be rude to the one board member whom he felt indebted to—Mike Markkula, Apple's first investor. He drove to Mike's house to personally ask him to resign. To Steve's delight, Mike wasn't offended. Like the caring man Steve had known him to be, Mike spent time with him and gave him advice about Apple: "You've got to reinvent the company to do some other thing, like other consumer products or devices. You've got to be like a butterfly and have a metamorphosis." Jobs totally agreed.

That August, Steve made his first appearance as the public face of Apple at the Macworld Conference and Expo (a trade show for Apple's products) in Boston. After a rousing welcome complete with standing ovation, Steve addressed the loyal attendees as he paced back and forth across the stage. He noted that this group represented just a portion of the twenty to twenty-five million devoted Apple users.

Steve listed what he felt was wrong with Apple and what was right with the company. He mentioned exciting new products in the works but told the crowd he wouldn't be introducing them that day. Instead, toward the end of his presentation, he said that Apple was part of an ecosystem, and it was necessary to get help from partners and, in turn, help other partners. With that, and the click of his slide changer, the giant screen behind him displayed the word "Microsoft." The audience booed. Steve went on to say that Microsoft had a good product. Then the laughter came because, as Apple devotees, they knew where Microsoft's good product had come from: Apple II's very own GUI-based operating system.

But then Steve took the crowd by surprise: He announced that Microsoft had agreed to continue providing Apple users with Word for Mac, and they were investing $150 million in Apple. Steve knew the importance of that investment. It would help keep Apple from bankruptcy.

12

RETURN ENGAGEMENT

THE ADDRESS OF APPLE HEADQUARTERS, in Cupertino, California, is 1 Infinite Loop. The word "infinite" means without end. What could be endless there? Apple's slide to failure or its climb to success? Steve wouldn't settle for anything less than success.

Just after leaving Apple in 1985, he told a reporter, "In order to learn how to do something well, you have to fail sometimes." Failure is an inevitable part of life, no matter who you are. No one escapes it, but not everyone grasps its lessons: For it's what one learns from failing that counts. Steve suffered his own personal humiliation when he was eased out of Apple. His two subsequent ventures, NeXT and Pixar, struggled for years to survive. Prior to Pixar's recent success, Steve had been labeled a failure in a very public way, throughout the industry and in the press. His every move was questioned and dissected—would he succeed, or would his singular, demanding, perfectionist approach be his downfall?

Digging Apple out of its financial hole was a daunting, but welcome, challenge. "I didn't return to Apple to make a fortune. I've been very lucky in my life and already have one. . . . I just wanted to see if we could work together to turn this thing around when the company was literally on the verge of bankruptcy."

In September 1997, when Steve returned to Apple (after a twelve-year absence), he immediately started a product review. He was shocked by the vast number of computer models being offered as well as the ones still in development. Trying to grasp the difference among the models, he asked, "Which ones do I tell my friends to buy?" No one seemed ready to give him a clear answer. The lack of response was proof enough that the number of products needed to be slashed. He told the staff they'd be cutting back from fifty products to ten.

With fewer products, the company needed fewer employees. First to go would be the ones he'd dubbed "bozos." But for the first time, he didn't like having to fire people, even though it was necessary. He found himself wondering whether each person had a family to support, or whether years from now, one of his own kids might be told they were out of a job. But Apple's poor health motivated him to proceed with the layoffs.

Apple needed to focus on a few areas only: desktop and portable computers, both for professional users and for consumers. Steve felt that now that Apple had a direction, many employees would welcome the streamlining of the company. In the past, they'd been stretched too thin and had worked in too many different areas.

Steve met with many of the employees and was flabbergasted when he saw some familiar faces he'd dubbed "brilliant" still working there. He asked them point-blank why they hadn't left long ago. Each one responded with a simple five-word sentence: "I bleed in six colors." The six colors referred to the colors in the Apple logo, and what they said meant they still passionately believed in what Apple had once stood for. Steve was incredibly moved by this answer.

With those dedicated people, joined by the gifted group he brought from NeXT, Steve felt the company could work wonders. He realized from his time at Pixar (as well as his early Apple days working on the Macintosh) that brilliant people, intensely dedicated, liked working together as a team. These A players, as he called them, could energize and feed ideas off one another.

While interviewing other Apple employees, he found one in particular who stood out: Jonathan Ive, known as Jony, was born in England in 1967. Jony first used a Macintosh in college at Newcastle Polytechnic, where he'd majored in design. He instantly related to that computer and felt somehow connected to the people who had designed it. Jony became a professional designer in England but eventually made his way to the United States to fulfill his dream—working at Apple. Ironically, when Apple hired Jony in 1992, the very person who helped create the computer that had impressed him was no longer there.

Jony was made the head of the Apple design team in 1996 but had been ready to quit when Steve arrived. What happened next, according to an industry journalist, was that "Jobs comes in, looks at all Ive's amazing prototypes and says, 'My God, what have we got here?'" Jony found that his philosophy clearly meshed with Steve's: The design of the product comes first; the development of the hardware had to follow to fit the design, never the other way around. In addition, both men felt that the design was not simply what one can see on the outside—it goes into the very inner workings of a device.

It didn't take long for these two visionaries to begin working together closely. "I think Steve Jobs has found somebody in Jony who knows how to complete or even exceed his vision, and do it time and time again," said a noted design consultant about the duo. Steve wanted their first joint venture to be "insanely great," with new features that would make it unprecedented and revolutionary: In place of floppy disk drives (which he never liked), Steve wanted this computer to have a place for a CD. Serial and parallel ports to connect add-on devices would be eliminated; instead the computer would be the first to use ports with the newly created plug called a USB. A fantastically designed mouse and detachable keyboard would be key ingredients.

Although a desktop, the computer would have a handle for easy mobility. Wires were to be consolidated, emerging from one opening. Best of all would be the simplicity of setup: The user could take the computer out of the box, plug it in, and be ready to go.

Ive said, "One thing most people don't know is that Steve Jobs is an exceptional designer." According to Ive, Jobs was involved with iMac's entire design. For many months, designers worked tirelessly—Apple wanted the iMac to be "approachable."

The iMac made its debut in 1998 on the same stage Steve had used for the introduction of his

Macintosh. As with all his presentations, Steve had been rehearsing for hours. He'd been screaming at the lighting technician to get the spotlights just so. Finally he whipped the cloth off his new creation: a gleaming, translucent blue-and-white computer. He detailed its "magic." And then, like its older counterpart, the screen displayed these words: HELLO (AGAIN). Having learned from past pricing errors, Apple set the retail price for the iMac at $1,299.

Steve was clear about what the *i* stood for. He knew that customers were clamoring to get onto the Internet, and this model allowed them to surf the web quickly and easily. He said that the *i* also represented "individual," "instruct," "inform," and "inspire."

The iMac certainly did inspire people. In its first three weeks on sale, 278,000 were sold. At the Macworld Expo in January 1999, Steve announced, "During iMac's first 139 days, an iMac was sold every fifteen seconds of every minute of every hour of every day of every week."

At the time, it proved to be Apple's bestselling

computer. People loved its look and its see-through case. What Steve had taken pride in all these years, a well-designed inside, was now visible to everyone from the outside. About a third of the iMac buyers had never owned a computer before. They were attracted to the colorful device, which was their first introduction to the digital world. Consumers were drawn to the overall ease of use and easy Internet access, with "more than 80 percent of all iMac owners . . . using their iMacs to access the Internet, with 65 percent surfing the web on their first day."

Steve also wanted the world to know that Apple was on the rebound. Once Amelio had left, Steve called his old friend Lee Clow at Chiat/Day, the same ad agency that had created the groundbreaking "1984" commercial. Chiat/Day was no longer working with Apple, but Steve begged Lee to pitch an ad. Lee, famous in his own right, didn't pitch ideas to get jobs anymore. But he, too, "bled in six colors" and met with Steve. They took a walk, Steve's preferred way to discuss business. Lee came back with an idea, one that so touched Steve that even recounting it years later brought him to tears. Lee's idea was to ask the world to "think different."

Lee and his team suggested that the essence of Apple's spirit was the people who used its products. Much like the company's two founders, Apple users saw themselves as creative nonconformists. Others would be attracted to this company for the same reason—to explore their own creative nonconformist side. Typically, Steve was involved in every single aspect of the commercial, which didn't show a single Apple product. He even did the voice-over narration for the ad. However, since Steve didn't want the ad to be "about" him, he ultimately decided to use a voice-over by the actor Richard Dreyfuss in the commercial that aired. The sole objective of the commercial was to bring to life the heart of the company and celebrate the dedicated people who worked there.

As viewers heard Richard Dreyfuss's voice, the screen showed many of Steve's heroes: physicist Albert Einstein, opera star Maria Callas, puppeteer Jim Henson, artist Pablo Picasso, designer and inventor Buckminster Fuller, civil rights leader Martin

Luther King Jr., and pacifist Mahatma Gandhi. On the final screen, the words "Think different" appeared just below the six-colored Apple logo.

The new iMac, and the ad, promoted the sense that the company was strong *and* innovative. As for Chiat/Day's campaign, it once again went on to win many awards for groundbreaking advertising.

But the success of the iMac didn't mean that Steve, the ultimate perfectionist, was totally satisfied with everything about the new consumer desktop. The original iMac had a pop-out CD tray even though Steve had specifically asked for an automatic-load CD slot. He made the designer promise the next generation of iMacs would have an automatic-load slot. The designer strongly advised against it, explaining that the wave of the future was to have recordable CDs so that people could "burn" their favorite music onto them. The technology existed for tray-loading CDs but not for the type Steve preferred.

Steve would realize that his decision had been a mistake. Apple soon found itself behind the curve of computers that could burn CDs.

In a little more than a year, Steve had changed the fortunes of Apple and its perception by the business world. As the twentieth century drew to a close, Steve and Apple were looking forward to the future, ready for its possibilities.

By 1999 the number of Internet users worldwide reached 150 million, 50 percent of them in the United States alone. And in 2000, approximately 60 percent of US households owned at least one personal computer. Across the United States, every type of business, from banks to hospitals, schools to department stores, transportation companies to restaurants, used computers to help run their daily operations. The Internet was surging, and in January 2000 the biggest merger in US history took place between "new" and "old" business when AOL (America Online) bought Time Warner (the largest traditional media company) for $165 billion. It was called a "company of the future" because everyone knew it was only a matter of time until books, music, and movies—really any form of entertainment—made their home on the Internet.

This was a period when music had a tremendous presence on the Internet. Even though it was illegal to share or swap downloaded digital music files, millions of fans did anyway, thanks to Napster, an online file-sharing program created by Shawn Fanning in 1998. At the height of its popularity, more than sixty million people worldwide used Napster, and it was obvious that digital downloads were the new and future way to distribute music.

Apple's next big leap was nothing short of transformative. Steve viewed camcorders, music players, cameras, and the like as part of the new "digital lifestyle" of consumers. Where did the computer come in? It was the "digital hub" that would connect all these devices and make them "talk" to the Internet. In 2001, when Steve was CEO, Apple radically changed how people accessed and listened to music. First came the software, in the form of iTunes, a program that allowed people to categorize and play digital music on their computer.

But then came the game-changing hardware: the iPod. Sleek and easy to use, it made every music player that came before seem like an out-of-date dinosaur.

Steve had prodded, screamed at, and pressured his design teams to come up with a music player. After incalculable hours of work, a handful of designers approached him with their absolute best effort. Steve looked at it, held it, jiggled it in his hand to feel the heft and weight. Then he walked over to his office fish tank and dropped this delicate electronic device into it.

The team members were dumbfounded. But Steve pointed to bubbles rising from the device as it slowly sank to the bottom. Those bubbles, he told them, meant there was air inside, which proved it could be made smaller.

A model that satisfied Steve was finally ready. The size of a deck of cards, just 6.5 ounces, it was ultra-portable and could hold a thousand songs, far more than any player on the market. Users twirled a "click wheel" to scroll through the song titles displayed on the screen. An entire music library of songs could be transferred to the iPod—using a superfast USB connection called FireWire—in about ten minutes.

Steve said at its introduction, "With iPod, Apple has invented a whole new category of digital music player that lets you put your entire music collection in your pocket and listen to it wherever you go. With iPod, listening to music will never be the same again."

But the music companies kept losing money because of the proliferation of file sharing. The federal courts shut down Napster because of copyright infringement, but the damage had been done. "When the Internet came along and Napster came along, people in the music business didn't know what to make of the changes. A lot of these folks didn't use computers, weren't on e-mail—didn't really know what Napster was for a few years," Steve said.

But Steve was persistent and returned to the music executives again and again. "Our position from the beginning has been that eighty percent of the people stealing music online don't really want to be thieves. But that is such a compelling way to get music. It's instant gratification."

At last Steve convinced them with the iTunes Store: a digital service that offered songs from all five major music companies for a small fee to iTunes owners. According to *Fortune* magazine, "The real buzz in the music trade is that Steve has just created what is easily the most promising legal digital music service on the market."

At its April 28, 2003, introduction, Apple's online music store offered two hundred thousand songs, with more to follow. Each song would sell for ninety-nine cents and could be purchased with a credit card, with one click of the mouse. A customer could either purchase one song or several or an entire album. The store also offered people the chance to sample thirty seconds of any piece of music for free. The ability to browse and search for artists and different musical genres opened up endless musical possibilities to iTunes customers.

At first this music store was available only for Apple users. But Steve had once said Apple was part of an ecosystem—they needed help from partners and needed to help partners in return. In that vein, he had the Apple team develop iTunes for Windows. He felt that not only was it the right thing to do, it

PATRICIA LAKIN

also instantly expanded the market for the iPod and for iTunes.

Just eight years later, iTunes Music Store has had almost sixteen billion downloads. Record stores are no longer the primary source for music. However, recording artists and record labels are in a better position to stay viable because of Steve's vision.

What started out as a financial mistake on Steve's part when he placed a non-burnable CD into his iMac led him to design products that brought Apple light-years ahead of all competitors, permanently changing the music industry.

13

"INSANELY GREAT!"

BY 2004, THE FORWARD-LOOKING Apple had continued to evolve. In 2001 the first Apple retail store opened outside Washington, DC, despite expert opinion that it would be a colossal failure. Steve disagreed with them. He felt that a magnificently designed space, located in a high-traffic area, artfully displaying Apple's products, would invite people to come in and play. It would be a toy store for grown-ups, with low tables, chairs, and computer games for children. Steve wanted the store manned by highly trained

Apple salespeople who could answer all questions.

For his first store, and all subsequent ones, Steve insisted on a clear glass front with Apple's logo its only identifying sign. Glass made a design statement, *and* people could see inside. Steve had liked the staircase I. M. Pei's architectural firm had created for NeXT's headquarters. He worked on his own "floating" glass version of that staircase. It became a signature fixture in many Apple stores, and Steve received a patent for its design.

Within ten years, there were more than three hundred Apple stores worldwide, with more planned. As each store had its grand opening, customers responded exactly how Steve had predicted: They came in droves, played with the products, surfed the web, and asked questions. Many went on to buy their first Apple product. Steve made sure the Apple experience also extended to product packaging. The design of the boxes that hold many Apple products was overseen by Steve and then patented.

"That's Steve," said Mitchell Kapor, the founder of Lotus Development Corporation (and designer of

Lotus 1-2-3). "He has an eye and a genius for design that cuts across disciplines. He was never formally schooled, but he has always had that sensibility."

In addition to Steve's considerable responsibilities at Apple, he was still the corporate leader at Pixar, which continued to have phenomenal success, with hit movies including *A Bug's Life*, *Monsters, Inc.*, *The Incredibles*, and *Finding Nemo*. Steve was a champion and protector of Pixar's independent, artistic spirit and in 2006 oversaw its purchase by Disney for $7.4 billion. As a result of that deal, Jobs became Disney's single largest individual shareholder.

Of course, success isn't achieved overnight. Certainly not the kind of success of a billion-dollar company with thousands of employees. As the CEO at a salary of one dollar a year, Steve was the innovative, tireless leader who charted and navigated Apple's not-always-smooth course. But he didn't do it alone: "We hire people who want to make the best things in the world. You'd be surprised how hard people work around here. They work nights and weekends, sometimes not seeing their families for a while. Sometimes people work through Christmas to make sure the tooling is just right at some factory in some corner of the world so our product comes out the best it can be. People care so much, and it shows."

Steve understood and embraced the knowledge that the world doesn't stand still. In the first decade of the twenty-first century, world events proved this time and again: Hybrid cars hit the roads; Hurricane Katrina unleashed its fury on New Orleans and the Gulf coast; the Twin Towers of the World Trade Center were destroyed on September 11, 2001; Barack Obama became the nation's first African-American president; the social networking site Facebook hit the Internet; and swimmer Michael Phelps won his fourteenth Olympic gold medal.

What else were Steve and Apple's team thinking about? Steve's thoughts, ideas, and aspirations offered some clues. In 1984, he gave an interviewer his vision of the next stage of computers: "It will be as if there's a little person inside that box who starts to anticipate what you want." The reporter reminded him of a prior wish: "You once talked about wanting a computer that could sit in a child's playroom and be the child's playmate." Steve answered, "Forget about the child— I'd like one myself!" Then, in 1985, Steve confided to another reporter who'd asked him about small portable computers, "Wait till *we* do it—the power of a Macintosh in something the size of a book!"

A little person—inside a computer—no bigger than a book?

That's what Steve, Jony, and a handful of designers and engineers had been working on since early in the new century. They were experimenting with multi-touch interfacing, a fancy name for scrolling or changing a screen's image simply by touching the screen with a finger. At one demonstration of this top secret project, Steve realized that what he was holding in his hands could easily be used for a totally different device—a phone.

At the time, some cell phone manufacturers were producing "smartphones," which did much more than make and receive calls. They contained calendars and sent and received e-mails. But none held music. Steve felt that a music-playing feature would soon be added to smartphones, and when it was, sales of iPods would suffer. He told his crew to shelve this "top secret" device. They could use this touch-screen technology to create a phone that would also play music.

At the same time Steve battled with his team to create the "insanely great" phone, he began a battle with his own body. In 2003 he was diagnosed with cancer of the pancreas, a gland whose enzymes help in food digestion. He was advised to have an operation, which doctors hoped might cure him. Nevertheless, he still believed passionately that adhering to a specific diet, limited to specific foods, was his path to health, so he declined the surgery. In 2004 Steve realized his approach wasn't working. He finally agreed to have the operation, after which he appeared to be recovering fully.

By 2005, "Steve Jobs" was already a household name. As such, he was invited to deliver Stanford University's commencement address. He graciously accepted Stanford's honor and wrote a powerful speech, one that has been praised for its simplicity and honesty. His speech, given in June, was two years after his cancer diagnosis and one year after his surgery.

He told the graduates three stories. The first, he said, was about connecting the dots. For the first time Steve publicly spoke of his adoption by his devoted and loving parents, Paul and Clara. He then told of dropping out of college but dropping in on an amazing calligraphy class at Reed. He urged the graduates to let their life's path be guided by their gut intuitions and their passions. If they did, they'd look back and realize how their own random "dots" or life experiences would connect for them in meaningful and surprising ways. As for choosing a life path, he felt the key was finding what you love and pursuing it passionately.

The second story told of his love for the work he was doing, his shame at being ousted from Apple, but how freeing it ultimately was. He said, "The heaviness of being successful was replaced by the lightness of being a beginner again, less sure about everything. It freed me to enter one of the most creative periods of my life." In addition to talking about starting NeXT and acquiring Pixar, he mentioned his wife and children as being an important part of this creative period.

Steve's third story was about death. He regarded it as a great "invention," for it cleared out the old generation and made room for the new. He also recounted his philosophy of using death to evaluate how he was about to spend his day. "Remembering that I'll be dead soon is the most important tool I've ever encountered to help me make the big choices in life. . . . Remembering that you are going to die is the best way I know to avoid the trap of thinking you have something to lose. . . . There is no reason not to follow your heart." He added, "Your time is limited, so don't waste it living someone else's life."

Not only had Steve *never* lived anyone else's life, he also didn't waste time. By January 2007 Apple was ready for its latest trailblazing debut. Steve walked onto the stage sporting his wardrobe of choice: sneakers, blue jeans, and a black turtleneck. Behind him was a huge screen, and in his hand was a slide-changing "clicker." Showman Steve Jobs told the crowd, "This is a day I've been looking forward to for two and a half years. Every once in a while a revolutionary product comes along that changes everything." He would be presenting *three* revolutionary products: a wide-screen iPod with touch controls, a mobile phone, and a breakthrough communication device. He mentioned these same devices several times, as the three icons spun on the screen and merged into one single cube. Then, humorously, he asked the crowd, "Are you getting it? These are not three separate devices. This is one device. And we are calling it iPhone. Today Apple is going to reinvent the phone." The crowd cheered. From that point on, cell phone manufacturers wanted to replicate what Steve and Apple had done. However, many of the phone's features had been patented, and Apple owned those rights. Lucky for them: Sales of the phone were more than 270,000 in the first two days alone.

At the conference, Steve also made another far-reaching announcement. "We're dropping the computer from our name, and from this day forward, we're going to be known as Apple Inc. to reflect the product mix that we have today."

• • •

By 2008, it was clear that Steve's cancer had returned. He was growing thin, he was often in pain, and he was running out of options for a cure. He took several medical leaves from Apple. But his heart and mind were always at work, checking in with Jony and his A team to assess their progress on a product he'd dreamed of for years.

On January 27, 2010, his top secret dream device was ready, and so was Steve. As usual, he stood on a stark stage, wearing his "uniform." Behind him the right side of a screen pictured a photo of a sleek Apple laptop. On the left was a photo of the iPhone. What device, he asked the audience, could do things not easily accomplished on either a laptop or a phone? The images separated, and a question mark appeared in the middle.

Apple had such a device.

The question mark whooshed away. Like a gift from above, the word *iPad* shot down and landed on a puffy cloud. Then a thin black-screened tablet appeared on the screen. Steve explained that the iPad has Internet and e-mail capabilities. It stores and plays music; it stores and displays photos and books; it's "right there, holding the Internet in your hands," he declared.

This was what Steve, Jony, and many others at Apple had been working on for years—even before the iPhone: "I actually started on the tablet first. I had this idea of being able to get rid of the keyboard, type on a multi-touch glass display. . . . And about six months later, they called me in and showed me this prototype display. And it was amazing. This is in the early 2000s. . . . I put the tablet project on the shelf, because the phone was more important."

But was the iPad simply a glorified phone or a smaller laptop? In reality, it proved to be so much more. From the minute it was introduced, software programmers were designing applications, or apps, for this device. Yes, there were games, but there were also maps, and apps that could actually speak—and speak in many languages. And iPad users kept discovering their own new and innovative ways to use it. "I think the experience of using an iPad is going to be profound for many people," Jobs told a reporter in 2010. "When people see how immersive the experience is, how you directly engage with it, the only word is *magical*."

When a young boy in France who was unable to stand, speak, or hold a pencil was given an iPad, he instinctively knew how to scroll. Suddenly he could play games, listen to stories, and interact with the world. He had more than a toy; he had a means to communicate.

Parents of autistic children, both young and adult, were able to see them interact, learn, progress, and make their wishes known through the iPad. Stroke victims used iPads to aid in their rehabilitation. Doctors and health providers used iPads to record patient notes or show them X-rays. School systems adopted iPads as tools for students, leading to a dramatic rise in reading and math scores. The iPad has been used to assist the disabled to cast their vote in elections.

In a 1985 interview, Steve was asked what he perceived as the future of computers. His answer was not specific. Instead he referred to Alexander Graham Bell, the inventor of the telephone. If Bell had been asked to foresee how the telephone would be used one hundred years after it had been invented,

Steve said, "he wouldn't have been able to tell . . . the ways the telephone would affect the world."

How will future generations use all the extraordinary products that Steve and his team created? Will the next generation be inspired by Steve Jobs to make "insanely great" creations that will put a dent in the universe? Sadly, Steve won't know. He died on October 5, 2011, at the age of fifty-six.

While his death was not unexpected, the news shocked the world. At every Apple store in the world, people gathered, left notes, and held up their iPads with a flickering candle on the screen. Many left an actual apple, with a bite taken out of it.

One young man, halfway around the world from Apple headquarters and Steve's home, created a graphic design that was viewed on the Internet and made its way around the world. He'd superimposed Steve's face, in silhouette, on the Apple logo where the bite had been.

On a piece of paper was this simple and eloquent tribute inscribed in Apple Chancery font: "*iThank you, steven p. jobs.*"

PATRICIA LAKIN

14

"THINK DIFFERENT"

N WEDNESDAY AFTERNOON, October 19, 2011, thousands of Steve's Apple family gathered in the atrium just outside the company headquarters in Cupertino. A gentle California sun shone on posters of Steve at various stages of his life, hung from the buildings. Tim Cook, Apple's new CEO, announced that Apple stores worldwide were closed so that every employee could watch the memorial service.

Could the life of Steve Jobs be summed up in an afternoon? How would he be described? Troublemaker, tyrant, dreamer, designer, creator, captain of industry, visionary?

Was Steve Jobs, as many think, the sole creator and designer of the products he so proudly introduced? Or was he like an ingenious conductor who assembled an orchestra of brilliant musicians and led them in playing his tunes, always to perfection?

Whichever role he played, there is no question that Steve fulfilled his dream to put a dent in the universe. While the most obvious "dents" are the actual physical products that were created and the changes they brought, there are also Steve's intangible dents: imagination, perseverance, passion, and daring.

Perhaps the most meaningful way to remember who Steve was and how he wanted to indelibly influence the world is to read the very words he recorded for the "Think Different" ad:

> Here's to the crazy ones. The misfits. The
> rebels. The troublemakers. The round pegs
> in the square holes. The ones who see
> things differently. They're not fond of rules.

And they have no respect for the status quo. You can quote them, disagree with them, glorify or vilify them. About the only thing you can't do is ignore them. Because they change things. They push the human race forward. While some may see them as the crazy ones, we see genius. Because the people who are crazy enough to think they can change the world are the ones who do.

sources

INTRODUCTION

Jobs, Steve. Commencement address delivered at Stanford University, June 12, 2005.

CHAPTER 1

Isaacson, Walter. *Steve Jobs*. New York: Simon & Schuster, 2011.

Lohr, Steve. "Creating Jobs," *New York Times*, January 12, 1997. http://www.nytimes.com/1997/01/12/magazine/creating-jobs.html ?pagewanted=all&core=pm.

Moritz, Michael. *Return to the Little Kingdom*. New York: The Overlook Press, 1984.

Morrow, Daniel, Interviewer and Executive Director Computerworld Smithsonian Awards Program. Smithsonian Institution Oral and Video Histories: Steve Jobs, April 20, 1995. http://americanhistory.si.edu/collections/comphist/sj1.html.

Obituary of Imogene "Teddy" Hill from the *Davis Enterprise*, September 19, 2003 (Yolo County, California). <http://www.davisenterprise.com/>; http://newsarch.rootsweb.com/th/read/CAYOLO/2003-09/1063990305.

Sheff, David. "Playboy Interview: Steven Jobs." *Playboy*, February 1985. http://www.playboy.com/magazine/playboy-interview-steve-jobs.

Young, Jeffrey S. *Steve Jobs: The Journey Is the Reward*. Chicago: Scott Foresman, 1987.

CHAPTER 2

Gromov, Gregory. "Silicon Valley History." http://www.netvalley.com/svhistory.html.

Morrow, Smithsonian Oral and Video Histories: Steve Jobs.

"The Nobel Prize in Physics 1956."
http://www.nobelprize.org/nobel_prizes/physics/laureates/1956/.

Sheff, *Playboy* interview.

Wozniak, Steve, with Gina Smith. *iWoz: Computer Geek to Cult Icon; How I Invented the Personal Computer, Co-Founded Apple, and Had Fun Doing It.* New York: W.W. Norton & Company, Inc., 2006.

Young, *Journey Is the Reward.*

CHAPTER 3
Brand, Stewart. *Whole Earth Catalog*, June 1971.
http://www.wholeearth.com/issue-electronic-edition.php?iss=1150.

Imbimbo, Anthony. *Steve Jobs: The Brilliant Mind Behind Apple.* New York: Gareth Stevens Publishing, 2009.

Jobs, Stanford commencement address.

Moritz, *Return to the Little Kingdom.*

Sheff, *Playboy* interview.

Wozniak and Smith, *iWoz.*

Young, *Journey Is the Reward.*

CHAPTER 4
Baba, Neem Karoli. http://www.neebkaroribaba.com/.

Brand, *Whole Earth Catalog.*

Isaacson, *Steve Jobs.*

Jobs, Stanford commencement address.

Lakin, Patricia. Descriptions of Ganges and New Delhi are based on author's experiences. 2007.

Langlois, Ed. "Communicating Word of God Is Oregon Priest's Passion as Calligrapher." *The Catholic Review*, March 21, 2011. http://www.catholicreview.org/subpages/storyworldnew-new.aspx?action=9690.

Moritz, *Return to the Little Kingdom*.

Schwartz, Todd. "The Dance of the Pen." *Reed Magazine*, August 2003. http://web.reed.edu/reed_magazine/aug2003/features/dance_of_pen/index.html.

Young, *Journey Is the Reward*.

CHAPTER 5
Sheff, *Playboy* interview.

Wozniak and Smith, *iWoz*.

CHAPTER 6
Moritz, *Return to the Little Kingdom*.

Wozniak and Smith, *iWoz*.

CHAPTER 7
Dernbach, Christoph. "Steve Jobs: Timeline of a Visionary and Creative Genius." Mac History, October 14, 2011. http://www.mac-history.net/.

Grannell, Craig. "An Interview with Rob Janoff, Designer of the Apple Logo." Revert to Saved, February 23, 2011. http://reverttosaved.com/2011/02/23/an-interview-with-rob-janoff-designer-of-the-apple-logo/.

Isaacson, *Steve Jobs*.

Moritz, *Return to the Little Kingdom*.

Sheff, *Playboy* interview.

Wozniak, Steve. "Apple Computer with Steve Wozniak." OnInnovation: Visionaries Thinking Out Loud, August 2008. http://www.oninnovation .com/videos/detail.aspx?video=1381&title=Apple%20Computer.

Wozniak and Smith, *iWoz*.

CHAPTER 8
Corrigan, Jim. *Business Leaders: Steve Jobs*. Greensboro, North Carolina: Morgan Reynolds Publishing, 2009.

Isaacson, *Steve Jobs*.

Moritz, *Return to the Little Kingdom*.

Sheff, *Playboy* interview.

Sorensen, Chris, Michael Friscolanti, and Jason Kirby. "The Life and Times of Steve Jobs." Macleans.ca, October 17, 2011. http://www2.macleans.ca/2011/10/17/thinking-different/.

Weyhrich, Steven. "Apple II History: The Story of 'the MOST Personal Computer.'" http://apple2history.org/history/ah05/.

Wozniak and Smith, *iWoz*.

Xerox PARC Visit. http://www-sul.stanford.edu/mac/parc.html.

Young, *Journey Is the Reward*.

CHAPTER 9
Corrigan, *Business Leaders*.

Future, Dr. "Memorial Interview with Dan Kottke, Steve Jobs's Best Friend." KSCO Radio, October 10, 2011. http://www.drfutureshow.com/drfutureblog /2011/10/10/memorial-interview-with-dan-kottke-steve-jobs-best-friend.html.

Isaacson, *Steve Jobs*.

Linzmayer, Owen. *Apple Confidential 2.0: The Definitive History of the World's Most Colorful Company*. San Francisco: No Starch Press, 2004.

Moritz, *Return to the Little Kingdom*.

Young, *Journey Is the Reward*.

Young, Jeffrey S., and William L. Simon. *iCon Steve Jobs: The Greatest Second Act in the History of Business*. Hoboken, NJ: John Wiley & Sons, 2005.

Zito, Tom. "The Bang Behind the Bucks, the Life Behind the Style." *Access/Newsweek*, Fall 1984. http://www.thedailybeast.com/articles /2011/10/06/steve-jobs-1984-access-magazine-interview.html.

CHAPTER 10

Berners-Lee, Sir Tim. "Berners-Lee Says Jobs Made Computing 'Usable Rather Than Infuriating.'" *The Guardian*, Technology Blog. http://www .guardian.co.uk/technology/blog/2011/oct/16/tim-berners-lee-steve-jobs.

Isaacson, *Steve Jobs*.

Lubenow, Gerald C., and Michael Rogers. "Jobs Talks About His Rise and Fall." *Newsweek*, September 29, 1985. http://www.thedailybeast.com /newsweek/1985/09/30/jobs-talks-about-his-rise-and-fall.html.

Nocera, Joseph. "The Second Coming of Steve Jobs." *Esquire*, December 1986. http://www.esquire.com/features/second-coming-of-steve-jobs-1286.

Price, David A. *The Pixar Touch: The Making of a Company*. New York: Vintage Books/Random House, 2008.

Sheff, *Playboy* interview.

Street, Rita. *Computer Animation: A Whole New World*. Beverley, MA: Rockport Publishers, 1998.

Stone, Brad, and Peter Burrows. "Apple With or Without Steve Jobs." *Bloomberg BusinessWeek*, January 19, 2011. http://www.businessweek.com /magazine/content/11_05/b4213006664366.htm.

Toy Story, Domestic Total Gross, 1995. http://boxofficemojo.com/movies /?id=toystory.htm.

CHAPTER 11

Corrigan, *Business Leaders*.

Isaacson, *Steve Jobs*.

Jobs, Stanford commencement address.

Linzmayer, *Apple Confidential*.

Lohr, "Creating Jobs."

Lubenow and Rogers, "Jobs Talks."

Simpson, Mona. "A Sister's Eulogy for Steve Jobs." *New York Times*, October 30, 2011. http://www.nytimes.com/2011/10/30/opinion/mona -simpsons-eulogy-for-steve-jobs.html?pagewanted=all.

CHAPTER 12

Apple Press Info. "Apple Presents iPod," October 23, 2001. http://www.apple.com/pr/library/2001/10/23Apple-Presents-iPod.html.

Cook, Tim. "Tim Cook's Speech at Steve Jobs Memorial," October 19, 2011. http://www.pcmag.com/article2/0,2817,2395161,00.asp.

Corrigan, *Business Leaders*.

Essick, Kristi. "The man behind iMac." CNN.com, September 22, 1998. http://articles.cnn.com/1998-09-22/tech/9809_22_imacman.idg_1_imac -macintosh-computer-today?_s=PM:TECH.

Goodell, Jeff. "Steve Jobs: Rolling Stone's 2003 Interview." http://www.rollingstone.com/music/news/steve-jobs-rolling-stones-2003 -interview-20111006.

Grady, D. B. "In Praise of Bad Steve." *The Atlantic*, October 6, 2011. http://www.theatlantic.com/national/archive/2011/10/in-praise-of-bad -steve/246242/#.

Grandy, Leslie. "Steve Jobs On What It Means to 'Bleed in Six Colors.'" Technorati beta, June 2, 2010. http://technorati.com/technology/article /steve-jobs-on-what-it-means/ [Speech at the 2010 D8 conference].

Isaacson, *Steve Jobs*.

Jobs, Steve. "Speech at Macworld Boston, 1997-Full Version." YouTube. http://www.youtube.com/watch?v=PEHNrqPkefI.

Jobs, Steve. "The First iBook Introduction," Macworld New York, 1999. YouTube. http://www.youtube.com/watch?v=cdpRSj7tLiY&feature= results_main&playnext=1&list=PL4E8296C1CDB29E44.

Jobs, Steve. "The First iMac Introduction 1998." YouTube. http://www.youtube.com/watch?v=0BHPtoTctDY.

Pearlman, Chee. "Who is Jonathan Ive?" *Bloomberg BusinessWeek*, September 25, 2006. http://www.businessweek.com/magazine /content/06_39/b4002414.htm.

Rao, Leena. "Apple: iTunes Now Has 20M Songs; Over 16B Downloads." TechCrunch, October 4, 2011. http://techcrunch.com/2011/10/04 /apple-itunes-now-has-20-million-songs-over-16-billion-downloads/.

Schlender, Brent. "Stevie Wonder Gets Way Cooler." *Fortune*, January 20, 2000.

Sheff, *Playboy* interview.

Waugh, Rob. "How Did a British Polytechnic Graduate Become the Design Genius Behind £200 Billion Apple?" *Mail Online*, March 20, 2011. http:// www.dailymail.co.uk/home/moslive/article-1367481/Apples-Jonathan-Ive -How-did-British-polytechnic-graduate-design-genius.html.

CHAPTER 13

Burrows, Peter. "The Seed of Apple's Innovation." *Bloomberg BusinessWeek*, October 12, 2004. http://www.businessweek.com/bwdaily/dnflash/oct2004 /nf20041012_4018_db083.htm.

Carter, Shan. "Steve Jobs's Patents." *New York Times*, November 23, 2011. http:// www.nytimes.com/interactive/2011/08/24/technology/steve-jobs-patents.html.

Corrigan, *Business Leaders*.

Fry, Stephen. "The iPad Launch: Can Steve Jobs Do It Again?" *Time*, April 1, 2010. http://www.time.com/time/magazine/article/0,9171,1977113,00.html.

Helft, Miguel, and Shan Carter. "A Chief Executive's Attention to Detail, Noted in 313 Patents." *New York Times*, August, 25, 2011. http://www.nytimes.com/2011/08/26/technology/apple-patents-show-steve-jobss-attention-to-design.html.

Jobs, Stanford commencement address.

Jobs, Steve. "iPad Introduction: Apple Special Event," January 27, 2010. http://www.youtube.com/watch?v=WLBQVKwcIDw.

Jobs, Steve. "Macworld San Francisco 2007 Keynote Address, iPhone," January 15, 2007. http://video.google.com/videoplay?docid=3206653149996743169.

Paczkowski, John. "Apple CEO Steve Jobs Live at D8: All We Want to Do Is Make Better Products." *All Things D*, June 1, 2010. http://allthingsd.com/20100601/steve-jobs-session/.

Seelye, Katharine Q. "Oregon Tests iPads as Aid to Disabled Voters." *New York Times*, November 16, 2011. http://www.nytimes.com/2011/11/17/us/oregon-tries-out-voting-by-ipad-for-disabled.html.

Sheff, *Playboy* interview.

Zito, "The Bang Behind the Bucks."

CHAPTER 14
Hormby, Tom. "'Think Different': The Ad Campaign That Restored Apple's Reputation." Low End Mac, April 9, 2007. http://lowendmac.com/orchard/07/apple-think-different.html.